Tuition and Financial Aid

A GUIDE FOR PRIVATE SCHOOLS

Tuition and Financial Aid: A Guide for Private Schools

Independent School Management, Inc.
1316 N. Union Street, Wilmington, DE 19806

Telephone: 302-656-4944
FAX: 302-656-0647
isminc.com
bookstore@isminc.com

Disclaimer: Independent School Management, Inc. (ISM) provides management consulting and other services to private-independent schools. ISM is not a law firm. No service or information provided by ISM in any verbal or written form (including this book) should be construed as legal advice. ISM specifically advises schools to consult with legal counsel qualified in their jurisdiction regarding all legal matters (including the hiring, rewarding, and terminating of personnel). All Web links and references in this book are correct as of the publication date, but may have become inactive or otherwise modified since that time.

ISBN-13: 978-1-883627-16-4

Contents

Introduction

Tuition and Financial Aid Are Not About Money.
Tuition and Financial Aid Are About Mission.

When consulting with a private school, Independent School Management always starts from the point of the school's mission. This foundational statement—often further clarified by statements of values, philosophy, and educational practice—distinguishes any given school from its neighbors (public and private). It enables each school to have purpose—and be competitive!—within the marketplace. We gauge each school practice or policy against this mission to discover its importance: "Does this practice or policy further our mission or not?"

Tuition and Financial Aid: A Guide for Private Schools introduces important management and leadership theory, as well as ISM research, that provides the backdrop enabling schools to support and sustain their missions. Given that school missions are about children (rather than faculty, administration, Boards, or others), the implication is that this theory and research answer the question about whether particular practices or policies are "good for children."

Tuition and Financial Aid does not—and cannot—tell you what your tuition rates should be. Nor does it tell you that a particular tuition rate is too "high" or too "low." The book also does not dictate how much you should earmark for financial aid. It does, however, tell you what the real questions should be and the considerations that will impact those questions.

Question 1: What is your mission?
Question 2: What kind of school will deliver your mission?
Question 3: How much money do you need to run that kind of school?
Question 4: How many students do you have to provide that money?

Tuition and Financial Aid is not about dollars and cents. It is about what your school is and how it communicates that to the secondary client—the parent. It is about what your school is and how it delivers excellence to the primary client—the student. It is about what your school promises through its admission process and how that promise is (or is not) kept in every program—from academics through cocurricular programs; through leadership programs; through the Business Office; and through development, constituent relations, and admission.

We hope this book inspires you to have meaningful conversations about your school, and take the tuition and financial aid actions that enable you to have a sustainable and mission-appropriate future.

Tuition

Price, Product, or Process: How Do You Define Your School?

Borrowing originally from concepts advanced in the for-profit sector, ISM has taught a basic competitive-marketing truth. Private schools can compete on the basis of price, product, or process, but not based on all three at the same time. The implications of this truth for strategic planning would be hard to overstate. As you, the Board President, prepare for your next planning event, take responsibility for assisting your colleagues in working from a marketplace stance that fits your school's competitive platform.

In general and simplest terms, this means that you can define your school as seeking to:

- generate the **best product** (defined here as seeking to be academically the premier school in your market, producing the academically best prepared students); or

– engage students in the **best process** (defined here as seeking to create a uniquely excellent physical and/or psychological learning environment, engaging in uniquely excellent pedagogical approaches, providing the greatest array of student curricular and cocurricular choice, achieving the lowest possible student-staff and student-faculty ratios, and/or other "process features" that set your school apart based on the quality, quantity, and types of things it does every day); or

– be *different* from those schools that strive to be "the best" by product or process measures. Schools in this third category can compete on the basis of their marketable differences and, *because their marketplace stance is so "different,"* based on **value and price**. That is, they cost less than those schools in the first two categories—"product" and "process" marketplace schools—because their priorities simply are not the same.

For example, a faith-based PK–12 inner-city school may cost a fraction of product- and process-based day schools in the same metropolitan area, including several whose "faith basis" (at least on paper) is not much different from that of the inner-city school.

Which school type is the best? The question has no meaning when worded in that way. The point of the distinction is this: If a "difference/value/price" school attempts to take on the characteristics of a product- or process-based school, its planning emphasis and outcome may become badly distorted. As a result, the plan would be expensive in ways it should not be. (Note, however, that your school can compete both on the basis of "product" and "process," but only at far greater expense. This will be discussed in the following section, "The Marketplace Taxonomy: Overview.")

For example, Trustees at the hypothetical faith-based school might, in a planning retreat, become enamored of a product-based quality (e.g., the prestige suggested by university-placement lists) or a process-based one (e.g., the student-faculty/staff ratios). To implement those qualities, the resulting plan may focus on "product" characteristics such as:

– standardized test score enhancement;

– beefed-up college-placement staffing;

– new approaches to evaluation of the college placement staff (i.e., evaluation on the basis of the prestige of university placements); or

– first-semester university student performance data.

Similarly, the resulting plan may focus on "process" characteristics such as:

– a third or fourth foreign language;

– an expanded personal counseling staff;

– various psychological and special needs services;

– more sports programs at more levels; or

– more and better-quality publications.

None of these planning outcomes would be "bad" *except that they have nothing directly to do with the school's competitive platform—its marketplace stance—and thus, may lead to a school that becomes less and less "itself."*

Now imagine the outcome if, rather than adopting the items just listed, this faith-based school set as its goals:

– renewed focus on a professional-growth-focused faculty culture, with the professional growth focus as much on the "faith basis" of the faculty culture as on strengthening pedagogy and research-based course content;

– fresh, faith-based approaches to the student advisory program; and

– renewed emphasis on quality and effectiveness in the weekly student and faculty worship experiences.

Implications

In which of these three categories does your school fall? ISM recommends that, in conversation with your Trustees and the School Head, you identify your marketplace stance using this three-category taxonomy. You can then carry that stance into, and through, your quadrennial strategic planning process.

The major ramifications are these.

- **If your marketplace stance is "best product," you must accept that your school will be expensive.** As implied by the discussion thus far, you will, for example, invest heavily in next-level placement programs (e.g., a college counseling program that reaches, in a PK–12 school, well down into the middle school). You will invest heavily in product-specific data regarding your graduates—both quality of placement and quality of performance.

- **If your marketplace stance is "best process," you must accept the fact that your school will be even more expensive than "best**

product" schools. As implied in the earlier example, you'll need the lowest possible student-staff and student-faculty ratios, an expensive arrangement in itself. You'll need the widest possible array of curricular and cocurricular offerings, both technology-based and not (e.g., extensive differentiation among levels of sports teams, numerous foreign language offerings, state-of-the-art-plus instructional technology, and continual attention to this aspect of teaching/learning). You'll invest perhaps less than the "product" school in staffing your next-level-placement counseling program, but much more in staffing your personal counseling program. You will invest in diversity—an expensive proposition unless your approach excludes socioeconomic diversity—and diversity-related programs to accompany your emphasis on the diverse make-up of your student body.

- **If your marketplace stance is your "difference" (translated here as "best value" or "best price"), then you'll need, in your strategic planning events, to guard assiduously against your planning colleagues' understandable eagerness to plan as if you were competing based on product and/or process.** Said another way, this means that in strategic planning, your efforts should focus on being "more yourself," with all the not-necessarily-costly types of differences that that entails, and not "like" those local schools that compete based on product and/or process. If you do seek to emulate them, you will inadvertently weaken your school's basic marketplace stance by making it considerably more expensive for the "wrong" kinds of reasons.

The Marketplace Taxonomy: Overview

Schools can compete simultaneously based on "product" and "process." Such schools may become even more expensive than schools that compete on the basis of one or the other. For example, such a PK–12 school would need an extensive next-level-placement counseling staff and an extensive personal counseling staff, rather than emphasizing one over the other.

In contrast, schools cannot compete simultaneously on the basis of "difference" (defined here as including "value" or "price"), on the one hand, and based on "product" or "process," on the other. Difference/value/price-based schools can be relatively inexpensive and yet, at the same time, do a superb job of fulfilling their core reasons-for-existing. But they cannot effectively retain that marketplace stance and simultaneously seek to compete with product- or process-based marketplace competitors on their own turf.

Consider the following table, which shows the kinds of dramatic differences in marketplace stance implied by the price/product/process choice. The hypothetical school depicted is PK–12 with an enrollment of roughly 700. The table illustrates, from ISM's viewpoint, *a theoretical, ideal level* of staffing, pricing, and facilities.

CHARACTERISTICS	PRICE	PRODUCT	PROCESS
Student/faculty ratio	16:1	10:1	8:1
Student/staff ratio	11.7:1	5.8:1	5.1:1
Tuition	$7K	$20K	$25K
Faculty	44	70	88
Admin/staff	16	50	50

ISM emphasizes again the core point: *No particular marketplace stance is "better" than another.* But to maximize your school's strategic excellence over the long haul, it is crucial to know "who you are," especially when engaged in your regularly recurring strategic planning events. The great dangers for the Board and senior administrators are these.

■ Strategic planners in "difference/value/price" schools may seek to have "product/process" features without understanding the expense involved, and the *probable loss of focus,* as well, in shifting to a different marketplace stance;

■ Strategic planners in "product" schools may seek "process" features without understanding the expense involved in moving to that marketplace stance; and

■ Strategic planners in "process" schools may continue to add such a plethora of programs and services that product (i.e., excellence of outcome) is eventually compromised through sheer overload and faculty/ staff exhaustion.

So, to recap, the **price/value focus** means that your primary (not your only) case for enrollment is your affordability. The **best-product focus** means that your primary (not your only) case for enrollment is your academic superiority. Finally, the **best-process focus** means that your primary (not your only) case for enrollment is that you offer more programs at more levels (i.e., more individualization) than do your competitors. There is more to be said about each of these, but those definitions serve as an acceptable starting point for this discussion.

A Further Refinement

Your school leaders must agree among themselves that their school operates—or intends to operate—with one of these three marketplace focuses. Now, let's consider modifications and clarifications of this.

Your regularly scheduled strategic planning and corresponding strategic financial planning event calls for clarity, as you move into the planning sessions, about your *intended marketplace focus*. If, for example, your core marketplace focus is your affordability, you will make a costly mistake if you add substantially to the number of student programs you offer or to the levels within those programs. If you do either or both of those, your expenses will rise sharply and tuition levels will follow. Your new strategic plan will move you away from your core affordability focus and toward the focal points adopted by schools in the other two marketplace categories.

Adding to your programs and their levels, apart from increased expense and tuition levels, places your school on the same playing field with the "best-process" schools (with which you do not primarily compete). You will move toward using their rules, their systems, their goals, their salaries, their faculty characteristics, their expenses, and their tuition.

From this one example, you can see the question of which marketplace focus is "best" has no meaning. The point of the three-way distinction is that—by knowing, understanding, and developing your strategic plan and strategic financial plan with a proper marketplace focus—you remain consistent in your approaches to staffing, expenses, tuition levels, tuition assistance, and all else that goes with those elements. The resulting plan will be a coherent expression of the marketplace focus that best fits your school's intended purposes and outcomes.

Consider the following table and its implications for your school, especially on your next strategic planning/strategic financial planning event, whether scheduled soon or several years from now.

MARKETPLACE FOCUS	ACCESSIBILITY	ACADEMIC PRODUCT	INDIVIDUALIZATION
Admission Selectivity	Values-based	Ability-based	Broad-based
Costs-to-Market	Low	High	High
Student-Staff Ratio	High	Mid-range	Low
Programmatic Focus	Targeted outcomes	Targeted outcomes	Breadth of outcomes
Outcome Characteristics	Best prepared for values-driven life	Best-prepared for next academic level	Best prepared for creating one's own path

Private schools can, in some marketplaces, compete simultaneously and successfully based on "academic product" and "individualization." Such schools may become even more expensive than schools that compete based on one or the other. For example, such a PK–12 school would likely need an extensive next-level-placement counseling staff in the upper school and an extensive personal counseling staff, rather than stressing one counseling staff over the other.

In contrast, few private schools can compete simultaneously and successfully based on "accessibility" on the one hand, and "academic product" and "individualization" on the other. Accessibility-focused schools can compete simultaneously and successfully, however, based on "academic product" and "individualization" *against other private schools within their own price range— that is, within the "accessibility" category itself.* Your accessibility-focused school can write its new strategic plan/strategic financial plan with the goal of achieving or keeping a "best product" or "most thoroughly individualized" stance *when compared specifically with other accessibility-focused schools.*

Whatever your marketplace focuses, your marketing materials must carefully circumscribe the claims you choose to make. For an accessibility-focused school to make the unqualified claim of having the "best academic product" and "most individualized programs" risks exposure by comparison with true best-product and most-individualized schools' standardized test scores and student-staff ratios.

Study your true competitors in the marketplace. Analyze their characteristics, using the ingredients in the table above. Decide your most advantageous competitive focus. Then launch your strategic planning/strategic financial planning event with confidence that your planning decisions will systematically strengthen your position in your marketplace—and help you as you determine tuition and financial aid parameters.

No particular marketplace stance is better than another. But to maximize your school's strategic excellence over the long haul, it is crucial to know "who you are," especially when engaged in your regularly recurring strategic planning events.

All private schools are niche institutions. Knowing and focusing your marketplace stance at all points—internal marketing, external marketing, parent education, faculty hiring and evaluation, attention to ratios—strengthen your strategic position. Choosing the wrong benchmarks (i.e., seeking to emulate schools with marketplace stances irrelevant to your own) and planning on that basis can do serious damage to your institution's ability to occupy its niche and remain competitive. Choosing appropriate benchmarks—e.g., other schools whose marketplace stance is the same as yours—may help you make the strategic decisions to ensure your school's mission remains alive and well for future generations of students.

Once you define your school and those it serves, you're better prepared for strategic financial planning—and a focused conversation on funding tuition and financial aid in a way that's fitting for your particular school.

Your School's Financial Equilibrium: The Three Levers

When the school's Board members and senior administrators get together for the strategic planning process, you must ensure that your school preserves its financial equilibrium. That's determined by three financial components. Imagine them as "levers," each of which interacts with the others.

 Lever No. 1: Your employee compensation package—salaries and benefits comprise a major portion of your operating expenses

 Lever No. 2: Hard income—your net tuition/fee figure, coupled with any earned interest (e.g., from endowment) and any "profit" from auxiliary programs (such as a summer camp)

 Lever No. 3: Your student-staff ratio—that is, the number of people who are paying you, compared to the number of people you are paying

That's it. Three levers. Deciding where to set each one may turn out to be a tough task, but it's not complex.

You set those three levers when, during the planning meeting, you and your colleagues:

- brainstorm your "ideal school" four to six years in the future,
- place expense estimates on all your new items (such as another secretarial position or employee benefit), and
- take a look at what this version of your school will cost to run.

That's strategic planning and strategic financial planning. Both done, of necessity, at the same time.

Tempted to name a fourth lever? Let go of the idea. That fourth one can only be "soft money"—that is, dollars that you solicit. It's risky business to build your strategic financial future around asking for money, as distinct from charging for your services or transferring earned income (interest).

Fundraising is great … provided you don't ask for money to pay for salaries, benefits, utilities, and other costs of running your school. Ask for money, instead, for enhancements or capital improvements and projects.

People will stretch their checkbooks to help pay for improvements that better the school—playground equipment, a software package for the middle school science program, uniforms for the softball team. Helping you balance the budget is just not an exciting prospect for most people.

Here's the thing: Those levers you set on your planning day work together. When you push one lever, the gears of the other levers move against one another. If your finances are roughly in equilibrium right now (if your budget balances without extraordinary assistance from your Development Office), moving Lever No. 1 forward (to pay for salary and benefit increases) means that Lever No. 2 and/or Lever No. 3 will strain to move to compensate. Otherwise, your budget immediately moves out of equilibrium.

So, if your school four to six years from now costs more to operate than it does now (a virtual certainty), just know there are two ways to pay for that, either:

- by increasing tuition/fees/interest income/auxiliary profit, or
- by increasing the number of students in each classroom, which shifts the student-staff ratio.

Everyone wants to set the levers to have the highest possible salaries and employee benefits (Lever No. 1), the lowest possible tuition (Lever No. 2), and the lowest possible student-staff ratio (Lever No. 3).

Here's how that equation works out:

High Compensation + Low Tuition + Low Ratio = Bankruptcy

Like all such algebraic phenomena, the equation is unforgiving. If you force one lever to move substantially in a particular direction and then do not allow the others to move in compensating directions, expect to glide down one of the slipperiest slopes in all of private school operations. Insolvency awaits your school, and it may not take long to get there.

Strategic planning is hard work—not because it is complicated, but because it demands courage from the planners. You must coordinate your vision of the "ideal school" with fiscal realities, and then make the tough decisions that keep the levers working in sync. That way, you ensure the financial equilibrium that allows your school to deliver its mission.

Dealing with Hidden Inflation

Involved in your school's budgetary concerns? Then you know that standing pat on tuition for a year results in lost ground. Inflation eats away the real income.

But it's worse than you think.

Many schools use the Urban Consumer Price Index (CPI-U) to determine inflation year-to-year. However, the CPI-U does not reflect expenses in private schools. It can only serve as a base figure. There are compelling arguments for adjusting your tuition at a rate 2% or more above the overall inflation rate.

The CPI has a built-in "productivity factor." It assumes the workforce is increasingly productive as computers, streamlined mechanical devices, and other laborsaving developments provide greater output with fewer personnel. Education, however, differs from industries in that it is people-intensive and not "product"-driven. Education cannot offset the total true effects of inflation by increased efficiency—the classroom still consists of a teacher and a group of students. If more students enroll, we create more sections with more teachers.

Even as the demand for more programs (and teachers) occurs, schools tend not to remove any of the standing programs to lessen the budgetary crunch. Costs increase even as productivity remains static.

Baumol's Cost Disease

All service industries—including education—suffer from a phenomenon commonly called "Baumol's cost disease."[1] William Baumol, renowned economist at New York University, developed data that showed costs in service-related businesses rise faster than those in product-oriented industries. This occurs because productivity in the labor-intensive service sector lags behind manufacturing, and salaries in the service sector must keep up with salaries in more productive industries. In short, the costs for health care, entertainment, insurance, law enforcement, and education always increase faster than overall inflation.

In service-related businesses, Baumol points out, it's difficult to reduce the labor content because quality correlates with the labor involved in the production. In short, to increase productivity, each teacher would have to teach larger classes (unpopular with parents and students) or teach more classes (unpopular with overworked faculty).

In an *Economics Letters* article, economists Xin Chen and Charles Moul reviewed the cost disease concept for U.S. public school education.[2] Although they review public school data, the issue is also significant for private schools. The core phenomenon originally identified and explained by Baumol (sectors with low or no productivity growth, like schools, must increase wages, and, thus, tuition levels, to compete with high-productivity growth sectors) places pressure on private school leaders to explain why tuition gradients exceed inflation gradients.

Chen and Moul found in their own study little evidence the populace recognizes that increased wealth is related to essential services from low-productivity sectors. Administrators and parents are as likely as ever to be skeptical that tuition levels must rise faster than inflation.

So, what does this mean? Private school leaders must take pains to make the case for elevating tuition levels at rates at least two percentage points beyond the increase in the CPI. ISM has research showing that school leaders in lower-tuition settings ironically need to work harder to make this case than will those in higher-tuition settings.

The Higher Education Price Index

Unlike the CPI-U, which is a "breadbasket" index, the Higher Education Price Index (HEPI) measures a fixed selection of goods and services that typically contribute to college costs. This includes professional administrative, faculty, and staff compensation; salaries and benefits for nonprofessional personnel; contracted services like data processing, transportation, supplies, and equipment; library acquisitions; and utilities. Although the HEPI could reflect some private boarding schools, it does not accurately mirror most private schools—college costs are not comparable to those in K–12 education. However, the HEPI is closer to the costs of private schools than the CPI, and reflects the service sector that Baumol discusses.

Over the past few decades, the HEPI has shown that higher education also faces a higher inflation rate overall than the CPI-U, supporting Baumol's theory. Looking back over the past decade, the rate of change for HEPI has averaged about 3.6% annually; the CPI, 2.4%. The costs for colleges and universities, like those of private schools, historically run higher than the CPI-U.

Getting the Word Out

Share the "2%+ problem" with your school's administrators, members of your governing body, and—especially—your parents. They must recognize that, to preserve the quality of your faculty and school programs, there is justification for raising tuitions to a higher level than the CPI-U. Trustees must also consider implications for endowment and other investments.

If your school does not keep one step ahead of real inflation, quality will eventually erode through decreased faculty morale, diminished services, and deferred maintenance. The 2%+ problem has not been adequately voiced—it has been an open secret. Now is the time to address the implications on your school's budget and take measures to correct any deficiencies.

---

[1] Baumol's "diagnosis" first appeared in his 1967 paper, "Macroeconomics of Unbalanced Growth: The Anatomy of Urban Crisis." For a detailed explanation of Baumol's "cost disease," see "What Ails Us," from the Financial Page of *The New Yorker* (July 7, 2003), available online at **www.newyorker.com/archive/2003/07/07/030707ta_talk_surowiecki**. See also Baumol's book *The Cost Disease: Why Computers Get Cheaper and Health Care Doesn't* (Yale University Press, 2013). Other books of interest include *Baumol's Cost Disease: The Art and Other Victims,* edited by Ruth Towse (Edward Elgar Publishing, 1997) and *Assessing Educational Practices: The Contribution of Economics,* edited by William E. Becker and William J. Baumol (The MIT Press, 1996).

[2] See "Disease or Utopia? Testing Baumol in Education," *Economics Letters* 122 (2014), 220–223.

Pricing, Affordability, and Accessibility

ISM has researched at length on pricing, affordability, and accessibility in private schools. In our studies of private school parents, most said they would or would probably keep their children in their private schools. With the majority of parents reporting that their children were receiving an excellent or good education, perceived value appears to be the motivating factor.

Parents leave a school when they think the value of the education is no longer worth the price. And to deliver the value parents expect, schools must adequately fund—mainly through tuition—faculty salaries, staff salaries, employee benefits, academic and cocurricular programs, physical plant, fundraising, marketing, reserves, and much more.

ISM has found no persuasive, verifiable evidence that private schools were pricing themselves into extinction. Money, with proper tuition setting, is not the game changer. The game changer for schools is adopting new technologies and teaching methods that focus on the student's individual learning experience to fulfill mission and solidify the value of the education the student receives. And proper tuition setting is based on understanding and acting on "relationships among pricing, customer service, marketing, and strategic planning."

ISM's Elasticity Studies and Sustainability

The results from ISM's tuition elasticity studies and parent re-enrollment surveys suggest the enrollment intentions of parents remains strong, and that tuition and enrollment are not correlated. Yet, many leaders continue to question private school sustainability.

From the many conversations, published articles, and association discussions that ISM has experienced, we note the following persistent "sustainability" concerns.

- "Tuition increases have outpaced inflation for years, and that is not sustainable."
- "Tuitions have outpaced the affordability of the middle class (or the middle class is being squeezed out), evidenced by increasing financial aid awards by private schools, jeopardizing their sustainability."
- "Colleges and universities are finding that most students are not paying the full price. Private schools must heed the lessons learned from this sector or face perilous outcomes."
- "We're not sustainable because our competitors charge lower tuitions (or are free)."
- "We must increase diversity."

Let's now explore and address each of these concerns.

Tuition increases have outpaced inflation. That private school (and university) tuitions have outpaced inflation is well documented. The real question is whether this leads to the demise of private schools. ISM believes the evidence of Baumol's cost disease (see the earlier chapter on inflation). Private school leaders do not need to be concerned that their costs outpace inflation. That is not to say that we discourage sound fiscal planning, prudent budgeting, and wise strategic planning. We think controlling costs is prudent and required. However, we do not believe that prudent fiscal planning will cure the tendency for costs to outpace inflation. We believe this is our reality, and that the economy itself, as Baumol describes, will correct the problem. And we concur with Mr. Baumol. There is too much hysteria over this phenomenon. Understanding the reality, explaining it to your constituents, embodying it through prudent strategic planning, and enhancing and communicating the value of your school's education are the best antidotes to protect our sustainability. But understand clearly, increasing tuitions above inflation is not a sustainability risk.

Many parents are likely to complain about any tuition increase and many are likely to apply for financial aid or scholarships. Before deciding not to increase tuition next year, recognize that wealthier private school families still have plenty of discretionary income. They will simply have to make lifestyle choices (like foregoing an expensive vacation) to pay for tuition. Educate parents about why any planned tuition increases are needed and worth any temporary sacrifice in lifestyle that they may have to make.

The middle class is being squeezed out of private schools. First, let's explore who comprises middle-income earners. Understanding the composition of earners is complex, and arduously debated. Some will look at the median income earner or median household income to determine middle class. Others argue that using deciles is a more comprehensive approach to understanding U.S. incomes. One thing is for certain: There is no agreed on definition of the middle class, and therefore use of the term is subject to individual definition. However, for our research, we used the deciles format. Using this system, the top three deciles, or top 30% of family incomes in the U.S., are those families that earn $80,000 or more (in 2012, when this research was performed). For our purposes, these families are high income, and the rest are either middle- or low-income families.

With this clear definition, the concern. that the middle class is being squeezed out of private schools is moot. The middle-income earners cannot even begin to afford the price of an individual tuition at most private schools (especially those in the "product" and "process" categories mentioned earlier). And even of the top household incomes in the U.S., only the top decile can likely pay the full tuition of multiple students. Therefore, the middle-class is not being squeezed out. Our schools are not, and never have been, accessible to middle-income earners, unless awarded financial aid. Further, we wish to make the point that middle-income earners are not the primary market for private schools. It's the top decile of income earners that most private schools must attract to assure sustainability.

Colleges and universities reflect a potential problem for private schools. The tuition dilemma at colleges and universities is also well-documented. Most students do not pay the full-freight tuition because financial aid is such a robust aspect of the affordability factor for higher education. The question we need to ask is a simple, yet often overlooked, one. Why do so few higher-education students pay the full asking price? The answer is also simple. Most students, regardless of family income, go to a college, university, or junior college on graduation from high school. And the government has built an entire financial aid model that reduces tuition for low-income families, and gives loans to everyone else. The market that private schools serve is sharply different from the one higher education serves. We serve the highest income earners in the country, those families who only qualify for loans in colleges and universities, not discounts. Colleges and universities serve the entire income demographic in the country. Therefore, the college and university dilemma is mostly irrelevant to the situation we face.

Our competitors charge lower tuition—and some are even free. First, it is critical that we understand the market that private schools serve. We serve an affluent market, one that wants a high-quality educational experience for their children, in an environment that is safe, controlled, and homogeneous. Parent surveys that ISM has conducted for nearly 40 years have revealed these facts over and again. Parents seek a private education for their children largely because of safety issues (ideological, social, and environmental). They assume high quality academics. When parents become dissatisfied at a private school, it is almost always because of lack of perceived high academic standards and teacher subject expertise, faculty who "don't know my child," and similar factors.

Schools often assume that families are leaving because the school is too expensive. And families will even tell school leadership this. However, when an outside interviewer gets the opportunity to drill into the reasons families leave, the affordability question is not the cost of tuition. The affordability issue is that the tuition is not worth it because the quality was not (high) enough. Or, said another way, perceived value was low. And further, ISM asks families dissatisfied with a school whether they would stay if the tuition were free. Almost unanimously, parents answer, "No!" ISM does not believe the data suggests that "free" is our competitor. Perceived quality is the real competitor for private schools. Schools therefore have to understand exactly who their paying population is, what they are looking for in a private school, and then build excellent programs to meet the expectations of that market. If a school does not wish to do this for mission-specific reasons, there is no shame in that. However, the school may face an eventual demise. This is not because parents don't want to pay private school tuitions or because there is a free option. It's because of differing values—what the parents value and are willing to pay for and what the school leadership wants to offer.

We must increase diversity. Diversity has been a significant issue in recent decades. Some private school organizations have even made this a compulsory goal. ISM does not believe that diversity is a bad idea, nor do we know whether any given school should seek any particular diversity. However, for schools that find socioeconomic diversity important, we want them to ask this critical question: How will our school pay for it? Perhaps a better question is: How much diversity can your school afford? The answer, not much. In other words, schools have limited discount dollars and this demand to increase socioeconomic diversity is a real enemy of sustainability.

The ideal strategy for sustainability is to fill every seat with a full-pay student, maximizing revenue. When a school cannot fill every seat, discounting seats is a good tactic to increase net revenue—as long as extra costs are not incurred for filling those seats. Schools have increasingly committed themselves, however, to the idea of socioeconomic diversity. This goal is, if not carefully managed, unsustainable. A school cannot continue to offer increasing amounts of financial aid for the sake of building an economically diverse student body. The goal, if achieved, will bankrupt the school. A school can use modest dollars, to a maximum of 10%–20% of gross revenue, for need-based discounts and tuition remission—but that is all. If a school wants a socioeconomically diverse student body, reflective of the real world, large amounts of endowment will be required to offset deeply discounted tuition.

The hysteria over private school sustainability is unwarranted. We should focus our time developing excellent 21st century-based programs, delivering high value to our families and running fiscally prudent enterprises. If we do this well, our futures are bright. If private schools fail to meet the high expectations of their clients, some schools may indeed close. But it will not be because their tuitions are too expensive. It will be because their tuitions were not worth the price charged. To stay competitive, private schools need not artificially hold down tuition. Their goal must be to continually improve—and to validate the strength of—their high-quality academic and cocurricular programs.

Affordability vs. Accessibility

Trustees, School Heads, and Business Managers often find themselves asking, "How can we keep our school affordable?" ISM believes this is the wrong question to ask if one of your school's strategic goals is to maintain long-term financial viability. The proper question is, "How can we keep our school accessible?"

Affordability implies that a school funds its programs via "guesstimating" what level of tuition its clients can afford to pay. This thinking further implies that a magic dollar amount exists—exceed that level and parents refuse to pay.

Accessibility, on the other hand, implies the school:

– funds its programs with tuition designed to cover operating expenses, and

– provides tuition assistance to families who demonstrate need.

This describes the driving force for setting tuition by what it takes to educate students, rather than determining parents' willingness to pay.

The hard truth is that most private schools are tuition-driven, realize little or no investment income, and need to discount tuition to their families to maintain enrollment. It is also true that tuitions increase each year (as they must), and do so in the face of any current economic insecurity. The challenge schools face is balancing these conflicting realities—providing a mission-appropriate education, funded by tuition, while preserving full enrollment.

This challenge highlights the importance of making sure that your school has a strategic plan and an accompanying strategic financial plan.

The strategic plan describes stability-related goals designed to ensure future programmatic excellence. Tuition will be affected by fulfilling those goals (at least those with implications for the annual operating budget). Future tuition increases (and concomitant financial aid) can be calculated from the plan and must be accounted for in the strategic financial plan.

The strategic financial plan ensures the strategic plan is financially feasible and realistic. An ambitious plan, not grounded in reality, can jeopardize enrollment and future viability. Without this vital document, tuitions are likely to be determined each year in a vacuum, without reference to improving the school.

However, even with an excellent, feasible strategic financial plan, it is still possible for your school to experience enrollment challenges related to tuition. Knowing what tuitions will be and believing they are reasonable is not enough.

ISM knows of no school that has experienced enrollment difficulty solely because of the tuition it charges. If a family feels that it cannot afford to pay a school's tuition, financial circumstances may be part of the reason. However, as mentioned earlier, an equal (or, perhaps greater) part is that the family does not feel the education is "worth the cost." The true question is not "How much can the parents pay?" It is "How much will the parents pay?"

Therefore, your school must constantly and consistently validate the education it offers, clearly demonstrating the quality of its programs and the attendant benefits to the students. Money follows program, when validated.

Ask yourself these questions.

- Have we defined our school's "competitive advantages"?
- Have we developed creative ways to show these advantages?
- Have we communicated what makes the education we offer different?
- Have we displayed the ways our students benefit from our programs?
- Have we educated our faculty and staff about their roles in relating to our clients?
- Have we tracked our alumni to:

  – learn of our programs' strengths and weaknesses, and

  – confirm alumni successes?
- Have we surveyed our current families to discover their opinions of our school (positive and negative)?
- Have we interviewed families who have withdrawn their children about their concerns? Have we considered those concerns and taken action, if appropriate?

Your school must maintain a proactive program of educating parents about the mission-consistent excellence of the education you deliver. If you are not validating this excellence (or, worse, if your school's education is not worth your price), expect tuition to be a continuing concern of your clients.

Now, let's get a little more technical.

The Dynamics of Flattened Tuition Gradients: Endowments and Other Revenue Won't Help

Some schools, fearing "unaffordability," have begun to take a price-averse approach to tuition (i.e., artificially setting tuition flat or below inflation). Schools turn to the teachers to "pay" for this approach and maintain programs. Schools freeze salaries or flatten their increases, reduce benefits, cut professional development budgets, and increase teacher workloads and class sizes. Schools know these approaches are only impactful in the short run—they are left to consider how their annual fund, endowments, and other revenue sources can help them flatten tuition. Here we show, through a simple equation, how these tactics to flatten tuition gradients are unlikely to be sustainable.

$$\Delta \text{ Avg. Net Tuition\%} = \Delta \text{ Expense\%} - (\Delta \text{ ORS\%} \times \text{\% Expenses ORS Covered}) / \text{\% Expenses Tuition Covered}$$

Where:

Δ Avg. Net Tuition% = Change in average tuition per student

Δ Expense% = Percent change in expenses (i.e., CPI+2%), aka "school-specific inflation"

Δ ORS% = Projected change in other revenue sources (e.g., annual fund, endowment draw, summer program, alternate business revenue)

% Expenses ORS Covered = Percent of expenses that other revenue sources covered the previous year

% Expenses Tuition Covered = Percent of expenses that tuition covered the previous year

You must accept, as mentioned earlier in this book: Private school expenses have and will continue, over time, to increase at a rate beyond inflation. Once you accept this unavoidable reality, the essential question becomes "What revenue streams can grow each year to keep pace?"

A school has three revenue streams: tuition, other business revenue, and fundraising (the latter two we collectively term "Other Revenue Sources," or ORS). The accompanying equation shows the percentage change in your tuition needed, given the growth in other factors. More important, it illustrates the pressure that school-specific inflation places on your revenue streams. (This equation assumes flat enrollment—which ISM recommends when creating multiyear plans—and, for ease of calculation, a balanced budget where revenue streams add up to 100% of expenses.)

Consider a school with a $10M balanced annual budget in year X. Tuition covers $9M and $1M is from a combination of annual giving and a summer sports program. Assume CPI is 2%, meaning school expenses are projected to increase at 4% (CPI+2%). We expect ORS increases equal to CPI. What percentage must average net tuition increase to keep a balanced budget? In our example:

on

on

Δ **Expense%** = 4% (CPI+2%)	= .04 − (.02 x .1) / .9
Δ **ORS%** = 2%	= .04 − .002 / .9
% Expenses ORS Covered = 10%	= .038 / .9
% Expenses Tuition Covered = 90%	= **.0422 (4.22%)**

If enrollment remains flat, you must increase your net tuition per student 4.22% to cover anticipated increases higher than the rate of expense increase. (And, if you give financial aid, you must increase the tuition figure even higher to compensate for the increase.) In our example, other revenue sources increased at a pace less than expense increases. Thus, tuition increases must not only account for the increase in expenses, but also for the other revenue sources that were unable to grow commensurate with expenses. This leads us to our first conclusion. To keep budgets balanced, if your other sources of revenue do not grow as fast as school-specific inflation, you will be required to raise tuition at even higher rates than school-specific inflation.

This is an important conclusion for those that fund their schools with tuition, fees, and annual fund dollars only. We know annual fund targets do not grow at CPI+2%, meaning tuition increases will always outpace school-specific inflation.

Should We Reduce Our School's Dependence on Tuition?

Some schools seek to be more "affordable" by reducing their dependency on tuition. They increase the percentage of expenses covered by development dollars and alternative revenue streams. There is risk in this approach. Suppose the percentage of ORS was substantially higher, and tuition was only needed to cover 50% of the expenses and 50% came from other revenue streams. We have:

% Expenses ORS Covered = 50%
% Expenses Tuition Covered = 50%
Δ **Avg. Net Tuition%** = .04 − (.02 x .5)/.5 = .06 (6.0%)

In this case, tuition increase would need to be 6%. So while the tuition figure will be lower, the annual increase will be higher. That this steep increase is at a lower dollar value is of no consolation to the family "on the bubble" for your affordability range. Conversely, if schools increase the percentage of tuition coverage, as in the following example where tuition accounts for 99% of expenses, average net tuition increases will better approximate expense increase percentages.

> **% Expenses ORS Covered** = 1%
>
> **% Expenses Tuition Covered** = 99%
>
> **Δ Avg. Net Tuition%** = .04 − (.02 x 01)/.99 = .0402 (4.02%)

This brings us to our second conclusion. *If your other revenue streams increase at the pace lower than school-specific inflation, then the best way to keep tuition gradients at their lowest is to have it cover 100% of your expenses.*

Can Other Sources Grow Enough Annually to Flatten Gradients?

To examine the growth potential of your other revenue streams, you will need to know your own revenue dynamics. However, consider the following.

Never project annual giving to increase at a steeper rate than tuition (even if it has the potential to do so because it was underperforming).

Traditional education-related programs (e.g., summer programs, academic assistance centers) suffer from the cost disease as well. Those streams have to account for their own expense increases. Progressive side businesses designed to fund your mission (e.g., akin to TOMS shoes, sales exist to support the true mission to provide for children in need), have been suggested by some as a solution. While this might be possible in rare instances, it can never be "the model" because it's not easy to repeat.

Many consider a large endowment to be a panacea for the tuition dilemma. Indeed, it has the potential to grow at CPI+2% or better. However, consider volatility that makes your revenues unstable. Even more problematic is that, because endowments only cover a portion of the school's total expenses, annual increases must be dramatic to cover expenses and the annual gap caused by holding tuition increases lower than CPI+2%. Now, let's go back to the equation. Imagine all other revenues were held to CPI, including tuition, in a school that has a large endowment that accounts for 10% of expenses and is the only other revenue source. What growth in the endowment draw would be needed? Solving for change in endowment:

Δ Avg. Net Tuition% = 2% (fixed based on desire)	.02 = .04 − (Δ Endowment% x .1) / 9
Δ Expense% = 4%	.018 = .04 − (Δ Endowment% x .1)
% Expenses ORS Covered = 10%	−.022 = Δ Endowment% x .1
% Expenses Tuition Covered = 90%	**.22 (22%) = Δ Endowment%**

Year One
Expenses = $8.0M
Tuition Revenue = $7.2M
Endowment Value = $16.0M
Endowment Draw (5%) = $800K

Year Two – If tuition up 4%
Expenses = $8.32M (4% increase)
Tuition Revenue = $7.488M
Endowment Draw = $832K
Endowment Value = $16.64M (+4%)
% Endowment Covers = 10%

Year Two – If tuition held to CPI
Expenses = $8.32M (4% increase)
Tuition Revenue = $7.344M
Endowment Draw = $976K
Endowment Value = $19.52M (+22%)
% Endowment Covers = 11.7%

A 22% increase in endowment draw is required to cover expense increases! Let's put some real numbers to this. Imagine a school has the budget figures shown here, and by policy, establishes a 5% draw on the endowment to cover 10% of the expenses in the first year.

In the second year, expenses are projected to be $8.32M, up 4%. However, examine what the endowment's value must be in Year 2 based on the two tuition increase scenarios.

If regular increases that large were possible, over time this would shrink closer to CPI+2% because endowment would be covering a bigger and bigger part of the annual budget. However, there would be some rocky patches requiring substantial percentage increases in tuition. This leads us to the final two conclusions.

- Relying on growth of other revenue sources, such as endowment or alternative sources, to keep tuition increases equal to CPI is risky because the growth necessary is steeper than we can typically expect.

- Even if you establish higher growth, the potential of volatility in those streams may result in needing greater sums of low-risk accessible cash. You may not have such funds available to ride out that volatility or risk high tuition percentage increases.

The four conclusions explained in this article affirm that keeping tuition increases artificially low places great pressure on your expenses and other revenue sources. Reducing expenses can allow for reduced need for tuition increases—but only in that year as it adjusts the costs down, but not the gradient. You cannot continue to add more and more students to the classes, increase teacher workload each year, or cut program. This is the crux of why Baumol applies to education—productivity gains cannot temper human resource cost increases.

ISM recommends a student-centric approach—determine what it takes to be excellent and create strategic plans/strategic financial plans to achieve this. If you are concerned about your enrollment, always look to your internal process first—not the external market. Even if a narrowing market threatens your school, being an aligned, dynamic organization that articulates and demonstrates the value of its program is the only way to thrive in an increasingly competitive marketplace. *Don't be afraid—be exceptional.*

Strategic Financial Planning: Implications for Tuition and Financial Aid Determinations

Your "strategic" plan is a Board-and-Head-developed document—perhaps three to five pages in length—focusing on the few ingredients necessary to improve your school's stability and solvency. It may include plans related to your major gifts program, to your basic marketing models, to your endowment-building process, to your Board-building approaches, to your master physical plan, and to your approach to operations finance.

'Strategic' Operations Finance

Develop the last-mentioned item of your strategic plan—operations finance—as a subset of your strategic plan. Assign this item the name "strategic financial plan" (SFP). An added page, for example, of a strategic plan might be a page of financial assumptions and numbers comprising your SFP for the next five to eight years.

Without an SFP, your school invites some or all the following negative situations.

- The annual tuition-setting exercise may be nothing more than a painful and often counter-strategic debate about "How much more can the parents stand?" Some of these same parents usually conduct the debate.

- The answer to the question is invariably "not much."

- The faculty and staff compensation package's upward gradient often becomes uncoupled from the tuition and hard-income package's upward gradient. Decisions on the compensation package are consequently shaped via another debate framed in language such as, "How much does the faculty need?" The answer, because most teachers are underpaid, is invariably, "a lot."

- The difficulty of managing and predicting enrollment and revenue is often obscured by wishful "predictions" of enrollment increase, and, thus, by a projected "balanced budget" whose assumptions are not conservative (a term synonymous with "strategic").

- The strategically crucial issue here is building and keeping satisfactory levels of unrestricted and plant reserves, and of continuous attention to their full funding. This often becomes lost in the confusion of asking the wrong questions in the wrong—i.e., nonstrategic—contexts of financially stretched parents, undercompensated faculty, and enrollment-management wishful thinking.

- Nowhere in the annual (if SFP-less) budget-building processes are the operative questions addressed: "Where are we taking the school long-term, and how will it be solvent when we arrive?" or, perhaps better, "How will the school arrive at its desired place without a strategic solvency framework within which to move?"

- If your school has undergone a recent accreditation visit, movement toward the visiting team's programmatic recommendations may, without a strong SFP, be undertaken with little appreciation for the often dramatic operations-finance implications.

Design your SFP in part to help your school "charge what it costs" to operate—i.e., to cover 100%, or nearly 100%, of operations expense with "hard (unsolicited) income." Without a properly structured SFP, your school may drift toward an ever-increasing dependence on annual giving and other noncapital "soft income" sources to balance its operations budget.

A Sample Strategic Financial Plan (SFP)

The sample SFP shown on page 41 is designed to assist a hypothetical—but not atypical—school. In this case, the school has drifted into a situation where its reserves are depleted, its demographics unfavorable for growth, and its class sizes small.

The school's programs are strong. Its leaders have worked hard over the last five years to expand the school's offerings (inadvertently reducing the solvency-crucial student-staff ratio) and to enhance the faculty compensation package. School leaders have tried successfully to hold tuition increases down because certain vocal parents and Trustees insist the school will "price itself out of the market" with more aggressive tuition increases. Much of the ambitious program-building at this hypothetical school has been accomplished in response to recommendations from an accreditation team's visit.

The school has, then, accidentally adopted an "insolvency equation." It finds itself in urgent need of the severe discipline imposed by an aggressively conservative strategic financial plan (i.e., aggressive in its attack on the "insolvency equation"; conservative in its assumptions).

The notes in the following list correspond to the numbered lines shown in the sample SFP.

1. Given the "unfavorable-for-growth" demographics in this hypothetical instance, enrollment is shown as flat for five years. (Note that, even with favorable-for-growth demographics, school leaders must bear in mind that enrollment growth enhances solvency only if the growth can be handled with current programs and staff.)

2. The tuition income line is a net figure, with unfunded tuition aid subtracted rather than treated as expenses.

3. "Other hard income" represents the profit from fees charged for auxiliary services and from usable (for operations) interest from the endowment shown on line 13 of the SFP. Consistent with the conservative thrust of this sample SFP, the "other hard income" line projects zero growth.

4–6. "Operations expense" (line 5 of the SFP) is shown to increase at a rate of inflation-plus-2.0% each year to strengthen faculty-focused operations funding in real (i.e., purchasing-power-adjusted) dollars. This number is shown subtracted each year from line 4—"total hard income"—to yield the "hard income profit and loss" figure (line 6).

7. "Hard income percentage coverage" shows the other mathematical relationship between lines 4 and 5 (i.e., other than the "hard income profit and loss" figure expressed by line 6).

8. "Annual (noncapital) fundraising" shows dollars raised by fundraising activities such as the annual giving drive, the annual auction, and other routine yearly solicitations. This line does not include capital campaign efforts. Consistent with the conservative nature of this illustrative SFP, this line shows zero growth for the five-year period.

9. "Overall profit and loss" differs from "hard income profit and loss" (line 6) via its inclusion of "annual fundraising" (line 8). Line 9 thus provides an estimate of the school's projected cash position at the end of each year.

10. "Annual to cash reserves" reports the amount to transfer each year into the school's unrestricted and/or plant reserves.

11. "Total cash reserves" indicate the unrestricted/plant reserves as that fund grows throughout the five-year period.

12. "Annual to endowment" refers to transfers of funds to the school's endowment, as distinct from restricted gifts made directly to the endowment fund (of which there are none in this conservative projection).

13. "Total endowment" begins at $1.5 million and gradually increases over the six-year period.

Now, let's focus a bit more on line 6, hard income profit and loss.

Your Strategic Financial Plan: Hard Income P&L

As you move annually through your strategic plan and its accompanying strategic financial plan, you may find the Board focusing on:

– the enrollment line (line 1A in the "Sample Strategic Financial Plan"),

– the net tuition revenue line (line 2),

– the expense line (line 5), or

– other meaningful lines within the spreadsheet's 13-line basic format.

Be most proactive, however, in teaching and reteaching the overriding importance of line 6 (hard income P&L). This line tells the most comprehensive and accurate story about your success in moving the school forward in ways fully consonant with your six-year planning document.

Sample Strategic Financial Plan

	Year 1	Year 2	Year 3	Year 4	Year 5	Year 6	Notes
1A FTE Enrollment	400	400	400	400	400	400	
1B Avg. Net Tuition	12,323	12,996	13,706	14,452	15, 237	16,050	Line 2/Line 1A
1C Tuition Increase		673	710	746	785	813	
1D Percent Increase		5.46%	5.46%	5.44%	5.43%	5.34%	
2 Net Tuition Revenue	4,929,230	5,198,430	5,482,379	5,780,737	6,094,837	6,419,931	Gross tuition less all forms of unfunded tuition assistance
3 Other Hard Income	333,266	344,097	355,280	366,827	378,749	391,058	Fees + net sales + useable interest from Line 13
4 Total Hard Income	5,262,496	5,542,527	5,837,659	6,147,564	6,473,586	6,810,989	Add Line 2 and 3
5 Operating Expense	5,364,546	5,634,482	5,918,516	6,216,252	6,528,966	6,851,847	Total operating expense, including debt service (interest and principal): i.e., all cash items
6 Hard Income P&L	(102,050)	(91,955)	(80,857)	(68,688)	(55,380)	(40,858)	Line 4 – Line 5
7 Percentage Coverage, 4 of 5	98%	98%	99%	99%	99%	99%	Line 4/Line 5
8 Annual Fundraising	250,000	250,000	250,000	250,000	250,000	250,000	All fundraising (not campaigns)
9 Overall P&L	147,950	158,045	169,143	181,312	194,620	209,142	Line 8 +/- Line 6
10 Annual to Cash Reserves	147,950	120,000	120,000	120,000	120,000	120,000	
11 Total Cash Reserves	750,000	870,000	990,000	1,110,000	1,230,000	1,350,000	Benchmark: 20% of budget
12 Annual to Endowment		38,045	49,143	61,312	74,620	89,142	
13 Total Endowment	1,500,000	1,538,045	1,587,188	1,648,500	1,723,120	1,812,262	
Sum, Annual Named Enhancements		Plus $109K	Plus $115K	Plus $120,181	Plus $126,226	Plus $127,012	

Notes & Assumptions:
Faculty Professional Development Budget = 50,000 | Benchmark: 2% of budget | Debt, Year 1 = 1,250,000 | Debt Service = 100,000
Line 5 Floor Gradient 3.00% | Lines 2 & 3 Floor Gradient 3.25%

Line 6 summarizes all the numbers that appear above it. It is the result of subtracting line 5 (operating expense) from line 4 (total hard income). The resulting number—always negative unless your school has reached 100% coverage of operations expense with hard income—shows how the Board and Management Team have been able to "manage to the planning document."

(Line 8 shows annual fundraising. Since fundraising is a joint responsibility involving management, Board, and the parent organization, that number is less under management's direct control than the first five lines and the summary lines 6 and 7.)

In some years, you will have moved some planning-document items back to later years, and perhaps moved others forward, as you set your annual administrative agenda (and the Board's corresponding annual Board agenda).
You will have adjusted the details of your expense and revenue lines accordingly.

No matter. Just "manage the planning document" by making line 6 conform to its original number, year by year, and your entire plan will remain workable.

Consider all that comprises line 6, including:

- – tuition-setting at each of your varying tuition levels;
- – unfunded tuition assistance decisions at each of those levels;
- – total FTE enrollment;
- – "other" hard income revenue streams; and
- – all operating expenses. These include employee salaries, employee benefits, professional development, and other kinds of expenses. Many expenses may not be under your direct control, e.g., inflation assumptions, service on your debt (principal and interest), utilities costs, supplies, and equipment.

Layered into those numbers are other elements in your strategic documents that have been calculated to increase your expenses, e.g., more noninstructional positions in several offices, or new equipment for some of your cocurricular programs. Educate your Trustees concerning the strategic financial plan that the real questions center not on enrollment, tuition revenue, unfunded tuition assistance, expenses, and other high-profile numbers. But rather that they center on the line that summarizes everything in the plan except fundraising (which, as noted, appears on line 8 on the spreadsheet, and is a shared responsibility).

Suppose, for example, that as you write the operations budget for Year 3 of your plan (refer to the sample SFP), a charter high school opens within easy range of your campus. Your enrollment—projected at 400 in the table—is now projected to fall to 380. This hard income decrease is about $275,000 (i.e., 20 students times the Year 3 average net tuition of $13,706, shown on line 1B). This can change your line 6 cash-negative figure of $80,857 to a cash-negative figure of over $350,000. In turn, after fundraising is added (line 8), this changes your "bottom line" (line 9) from six-figure cash-positive to six-figure cash-negative.

With the help of your Business Manager and the Finance Committee Chair, teach your Trustees to focus less on lines 1A (enrollment), 2 (net tuition revenue), and 5 (operating expense), and more on line 6 (hard income P&L). Then your school has a more straightforward task in relating your decisions in upcoming Board meetings. You may decide, for example, to announce the following.

- You will postpone adding noninstructional positions in two offices, reducing planned new expense by $80,000 in salary and benefits.

- You will postpone an increase in the equipment line(s) in support of three of the middle school cocurricular programs, reducing new-program expense by another $40,000.

- The net effects of these two steps will bring the line 6 negative figure to approximately $235,000. Coupled with the annually projected $250,000 in non-capital-campaign fundraising, this brings the "bottom line" (line 9) figure back into the black by roughly $15,000.

As the Year 3 fall semester develops and projected enrollment figures for Year 4 begin to harden, make recommendations as part of the Year 4 operating budget proposal. Determine further steps required to restore the 3% bottom-line margin projected on the spreadsheet for Year 4 (the line 9 figure of $181,312 divided by the line 5 figure of $6,216,252). If by December of Year 3, it appears the Year 3 enrollment figure of 380 (versus the strategic plan's projection of 400) will persist into Year 4 and perhaps beyond, adjustments in the projected net tuition gradient, the employee salary increase gradient, and/or the total number of funded faculty and staff positions may need to change, and to change substantially. *Your goal is to restore the integrity of line 6, so the overall operating budget will run the projected 3% margins. This, in turn, allows cash reserves (line 11) to drive toward the ISM benchmark figure of 20% of the operations budget.*

Trustees naturally think about "controlling expenses" (line 5 in the sample SFP). With your Business Manager and Finance Chair, help all Trustees to focus on the real strategic number—the number that expresses the relationship between expenses and total hard income. Expenses may run higher or lower than the numbers projected on the multiyear strategic financial spreadsheet. That is not in itself an issue, as long as expenses maintain a consistent relationship with total hard income. Line 6 expresses that relationship.

The Moral Costs of Private Schools

Many schools, especially religious schools, view their widespread dismay about rising costs as less of a "money issue" and more one of "moral costs." Administrators fear that parents feel they are being increasingly forced into an impossible-to-solve conundrum: financially ruinous tuition levels for their children, on the one hand, and their deeply felt moral religious beliefs on the other.

ISM provides advice and counsel based on those schools' commonalities with other kinds of private schools, noting (and often reinforcing) whatever pertinent anomalies exist on a case-by-case basis. We offer several observations that may be of general interest. The moral-cost argument can indeed be a central one for Trustees, administrators, and private school communities in general. Couch the argument in broader terms than the rising costs of tuition itself.

The following could be usefully viewed as "moral numbers":

1. Tuition levels;
2. Tuition-assistance levels;
3. Employee salaries;
4. Employee benefits;
5. Employee professional-development funding levels;
6. Student-staff ratios; and
7. Faculty-administration ratios.

Considering the "three levers" we mentioned earlier, these items connect to one another by mechanisms that are "under the floor and out of sight." Touch one of these variables and the others attempt metaphorically to "move on their own" to keep the operations budget in equilibrium. *Thus, if one of these has a moral component, then so do they all.*

For example, tuition levels (No. 1 in the list) connect necessarily to employee salaries (No. 3). Remuneration for one's faculty can also be considered a moral issue. If a low salary forces a gifted teacher to take a weekend or an evening part-time job, and if her teaching performance and her health suffer as a result, the consequences go beyond money itself. If poor salaries prevent a given school from attracting the best and most mission-appropriate teachers, the student experience will be impoverished. This result goes well beyond the question of money (which, in this example, deals with reaching and upholding enrollment levels needed to drive revenues which, in turn, equal or exceed expenses).

In teaching strategic planning concepts and practices, ISM emphasizes the "three levers" we mentioned earlier—net tuition, employee compensation, student-staff ratios (a compressing of the seven-item list into three for ease of discussion). These will always be set at compromise points. Tuition will always be higher than ideal. Compensation will always be lower than ideal. Student-staff ratios (especially as reflected in class sizes and in noninstructional services to students and parents) will always be higher than ideal. Thus it is that ISM emphasizes the two qualities most needed in strategic planning: wisdom and courage.

Add a third quality—patience—here. No strategic plan can instantaneously address all seven variables. But a strategic plan can set a direction to move the school toward its goal: financial stability that is sustainable and morally responsible, honoring each of the seven "moral numbers" consistent with the school's essential purposes and outcomes.

The Budget Cycle

You should work on and work from budgets continuously. As you follow and update your current budget, next year's budget should take form in systematic steps.

ISM recommends the fiscal year span July through June. This incorporates the school year, accommodates new administrative personnel as they join your school in the summer, readily records new tuition money, and allows accountants to review the school year during the summer break.

The Four Phases of the Budget Cycle

Phase One—Early Fall: Decide on the three key elements of a school budget (tuition and fees, salary expense, and enrollment projections) early in the process. The money available for salaries determines what positions to fill and at what cost.

Because administrators are essential to leadership, their contracts ought to be completed first. (If an administrator is not going to renew, you need to know early to have your choice of a replacement.) And new applicant families appear shortly after the holidays. They want to know tuition and fees charges.

You know as much about projections and other factors in October as you will in February. By doing budget homework and committee work in late October and November, you should be ready for approval of key budget elements by late November or early December.

Tuition announcements for the following year can then be printed in December and distributed in January—well before any requests for families to re-enroll. Meanwhile, complete salary discussions with administrators in December.

Phase Two—Late Winter: Develop a formal trial budget in late February and early March. This involves requests from departments, policy creation by your administration, and agreements on departmental requests. It should be detailed, well-documented, and fully participatory.

This effort occurs when personnel should be thinking through their programs for the following year and costing out plans for approval. The trial budget that emerges serves as a basis for ordering essential equipment and supplies that cannot wait for a more complete budget phase.

If the work done now is carefully prepared with priorities identified in various subsections, there should be little concern about necessary changes in later phases if income is less than expected.

Phase Three—May: Rework your trial budget based on the best data now available. (The current year's operation is at a close—and next year's enrollment should be clear.) Results should be discussed and approved by any advisory or governing body in June.

This forms your initial operating budget. It also provides authorization for the summer operation. In other words, it becomes the operating budget for the first three months of the new fiscal year.

Phase Four—September: Again the budget undergoes careful review—and possible major adjustment—once the school year is under way in September. Now specific items are known that could only have been projected previously: enrollment, all salaries, and expense and income accrued from the summer operation. The result is a general operating budget for the rest of the school year.

Designing Tuition Increases: The fundamental pricing concept held by ISM is: *Charge what it costs* to operate the core programs and services that you consider essential to your mission. Do not charge less, even though such a policy has become the norm for private schools. We have yet to see a school with quality programs and services develop marketing problems because of pricing tied to costs.

If your current tuition total is well below the amount needed to operate the school, put together a multiyear solution, perhaps for four years. Consider the following example.

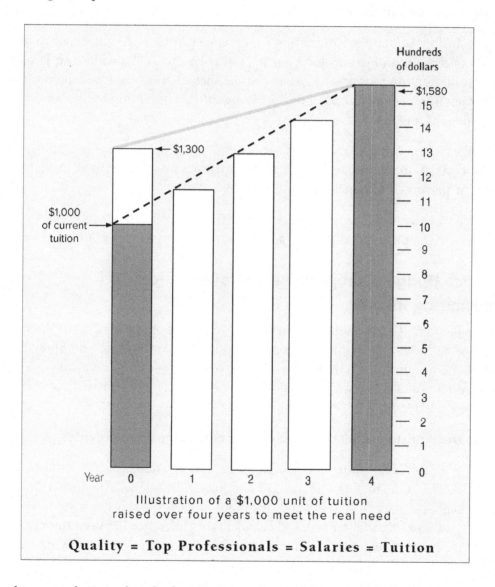

Hundreds of dollars

$1,580

$1,300

$1,000 of current tuition

Year 0   1   2   3   4

Illustration of a $1,000 unit of tuition
raised over four years to meet the real need

Quality = Top Professionals = Salaries = Tuition

In this case, the Board and administration decided that every $1,000 unit of current tuition is $300 less than that needed to pay for the programs and services essential to the school's mission. In short, the $1,000 unit should be $1,300 now.

If we recast the $1,300 by our estimated rate of inflation (3%) and increase it by the 2%+ factor (for a total of 5%) in each of four successive years, it becomes $1,580 in the fourth year. (Follow the shaded line from the top of column 0 to column 4.) This results in the dotted path that shows the change that each $1,000 of the current tuition must take to reach the goal in four years.

Of course, you could use one or two more or fewer years, depending on the amount you need to make up.

In conclusion, undertake fundraising for enhancements. Don't fundraise to fill a gap between tuition income and your operating budget. Gifts will be far larger and far more numerous when donors can see their money improves the program or the environment—instead of disappearing into an operating budget that remains unchanged.

As you examine your programs and services for core quality, keep in mind the major costs of quality programs include compensation sufficient to attract and hold the personnel that make programs great.

About 85% of your budget is expended in salaries and related benefits, and most of this goes to the professionals who lead and deliver your programs and services.

Reduce Budget Compromises: Strategies for Maximizing Income

As the Board and Management Team tackle each year's operating budget, they struggle with the challenge of supporting quality, mission-appropriate programs with finite resources. The budget development process is about compromises. In your search for effective ways to maximize income and ensure financial stability, ask these 11 questions.

1. Does tuition reflect the full cost of educating our students?

With tuition as your school's main source of revenue, the closer tuition dollars come to covering the cost of educating students, the greater the school's financial stability and flexibility. Review the school's most recent year-end financial reports and calculate the difference between tuition income and expenses. Is there a shortfall? Even if the gap is growing by only a fraction of a percentage point a year, you are setting an unhealthy trend. Build a correction into your strategic financial plan designed to close the gap quickly.

2. Do we adhere to a specified allocation for financial aid?

In each year's operating budget, dedicate a specific dollar amount to financial aid. Usually all of these funds are awarded before summer. Allocating extra "discount dollars" for late applicants will have an adverse effect on the bottom line, right?

Wrong! Offering enrollment to a late applicant, even at half tuition, increases income. View financial aid as revenue rather than as an expense. From that perspective, extra assistance—awarded after the budget is set and to fill a vacant seat—is unexpected (and welcome) income.

3. Do we set tuition at a single level across all grades?

Base this concept on the fact that your school offers a complete educational program rather than a series of discrete, grade-by-grade experiences. The benefits of an education at your school are realized over the full scope of the program. And so are the costs.

Some students who start your school's program will not complete it. As a result, you lose revenue by undercharging at the entry grades and increasing the cost as the student progresses. Flattening tuition eliminates this risk.

You also remove the "double whammy." When parents face a major between-divisions jump in tuition, besides the basic grade-to-grade increase, this "double whammy" may make them pause and reassess whether your school is still worth the cost. Flat tuition eliminates this challenge and allows families to plan their budgets more effectively.

One downside to flat tuition is that your starting cost may be higher than what competing schools are charging. Be prepared to explain the long-term benefits of this approach, educating parents about the breadth of your program and the value of experiencing all aspects of it from the first grade to the last.

4. Do we give automatic tuition discounts to families with more than one child in the school?

As a way to encourage families to enroll multiple students (as long as they are mission-appropriate), you may charge full tuition for the first and offer discounts to siblings. Your goal is to make your school more affordable to families who might struggle financially. However, consider that you are also extending this benefit even to wealthy parents who could easily afford the tuition. Does subsidizing your school's education for these families constitute fiscal responsibility?

If you decide to cancel multichild discounts, grandfather in those who currently receive them and discontinue the program. For families who cannot afford to pay full tuition for their enrolled children, offer need-based financial aid.

Again, you face a marketing challenge if you are working hard to build enrollment. If prospective parents weigh a competing school's automatic discount against your complex financial aid form, which will they choose? Check with other schools in your area. They may be just as interested as you are in switching from subsidies to financial aid. Or you might take intermediate steps, such as reducing the amount of the discount and/or offering a reduction only after the first two siblings have enrolled.

5. Do we automatically give our faculty tuition remission for their children?

The same logic that applies to the multichild discount applies here. You subsidize your school's education for faculty who can afford the tuition. In addition, you provide a substantially more lucrative compensation package for all teachers whose children are enrolled with you.

The costs of educating a student do not change. The issue is need. The most effective strategy is to give teachers priority and guarantee financial aid, up to 100% of demonstrated need, for the mission-appropriate children of all teachers who qualify.

This decision constitutes a challenge if tuition remission plays a key role in your ability to recruit and retain good teachers in today's challenging market. However, take a close look at how many teachers it currently affects, and for how long. Consider how many applicants ask about tuition remission. The consequences of "retiring" this program may not be as severe as you anticipate.

You may not want to cut out tuition remission entirely. One approach would be to gradually reduce the percentage so that teachers receive, for example, 80% remission next year, 60% the following year, and eventually phase out the program.

6. Do we require payment of all tuition before the beginning of the school year?

Sending tuition bills and collecting payments once a year makes the accounts receivable function in the Business Office more efficient. It also guarantees that you receive the full tuition from every student, even the one who withdraws in the middle of the year.

Again, look at the broader picture. Payment plans set your school's educational program up as a pay-as-you-go proposition. However, the cost of educating a student is all but fixed, from teachers' salaries to utilities. Those expenses do not change if a student withdraws, and you lose money if you cannot fill the vacancy. While you may decide to grant a refund under certain circumstances, the school, not the parent, needs to be in charge.

The best possible scenario is to collect all tuition by early August. Parents who cannot afford prepayment can take advantage of loan programs.

If you do not want to eliminate payment plans completely, reduce the number you offer to one or two. Collect a substantial percentage of the tuition as early in the year as possible, and do not allow following payments to stretch out until the end of the school year.

7. Do we levy penalties for late tuition payments?

Late tuition payments cost your school money. Personnel must review the accounts receivable, send more bills, and record the payments when they are received, disrupting the normal time sequence. Institute a late fee that fully covers the costs (both hidden and obvious) associated with collecting late payments. If your fee was set several years ago, make sure it covers the current costs.

8. Do we make the most of our school's cash balance?

When you receive significant tuition income before the beginning of the academic year, there are times when the cash balance far exceeds cash flow needs. What happens with those funds? Are they being invested? Is their interest income potential being maximized without exposing the school to risk? Work with the Board's Finance Committee (and/or Investment Committee) to explore possible safe investment vehicles and determine which ones are most productive for your school.

9. Do our auxiliary programs provide reasonable returns?

No auxiliary program (food service, extended day, summer program) should run at a loss. Review the full cost of each one, including hidden expenses such as utilities and wear and tear on the facility.

If a program is not profitable, restructure it so that it makes money or discontinue it. If it is turning a profit, ask these questions: Are we realizing maximum income from this program? Can the program be enhanced? Expanded to serve more people?

For example, the kitchen is used only a fraction of the school day. Could breakfast be served to students and their parents? Could the kitchen staff cater (and charge for) meals on nights when there are parent meetings? Could parents order box dinners to get when they pick up their children? Could the kitchen cater off-campus events?

10. Do we rent our facilities?

School buildings can sit unused for portions of the day, both during the school year and the summer. Renting the auditorium to the community theater, the gymnasium to a recreational basketball league, or the chapel to alumni for weddings can generate significant income. In calculating overall profitability, remember to include in the expense column the costs of insurance, increased utilities, custodial personnel overtime, and impact on the facility.

11. Are certain grade levels under enrolled?

Somewhere in the middle of a division, there may be a grade that has vacancies. These spots can be difficult to fill because families are not likely to consider changing schools before the division break. However, you can make an effort to reach new families and those who are dissatisfied with their current school, public or private.

Ask your marketing specialist to develop an advertisement that targets that specific grade level. ("Join the third-grade readers, writers, actors, math whizzes, painters, and all-around great kids at I&P Academy. Only a couple of spots left!") The hidden bonus is that you'll attract applicants for other grades as well.

You may need to earmark more need-based financial aid with this effort. (See the chapters at the end of this book for advice concerning financial aid.)

Budgeting is a series of compromises, as you balance program needs and desires with financial realities. When you adopt some or all of these strategies for maximizing income, you help ensure the compromises you must make will be relatively minor ones.

Don't Pay Today's Bills with Tomorrow's Income

It's an easy trap to fall into. The fiscal year ends in three months, and your school's income doesn't cover expenses. Since families have already made a tuition deposit for next year, why not "borrow" just enough to cover the deficit?

It may seem like a small matter now, but over time this short-term solution can threaten your school's long-term financial stability.

As an example, take a look at what happened when I&P Academy—our fictitious K–12 coed day school—tried using this approach to deal with its financial situation.

The chart on page 57 shows how I&P Academy's debt increased over a four-year period.

In Year A, I&P Academy's expenses and income matched. Tuition deposits were received in advance and invested, so the expenses for Year A were covered in full by tuition deposits, plus interest earned, plus tuition payments. At the end of the year, there was neither a surplus nor a deficit.

In Year B, though, I&P Academy fell short of meeting expenses by 12.5%, because of a series of unforeseen events. One teacher became ill and another left the school. Hiring long-term substitutes to take their places exceeded the budget line. Then the heating system needed emergency repairs.

I&P Academy could not cut other expenses enough to cover the shortfall. Coincidentally, tuition deposits already received for Year C equaled the shortage in income. It seemed like the perfect short-term solution, even though that income should have been held to pay Year C expenses.

As a result, Year C brought an accumulated deficit of 25% (12.5% from Year B and 12.5% from Year C). It was only because of "good fortune" that the school met its basic expenses. Parents not only paid their enrollment deposits for the coming year, but several chose to prepay their entire tuitions.

I&P Academy "borrowed" that extra advance income just to meet the increased expenses, and the deficit continued to grow.

In Year D, the original 12.5% deficit grew to 37.5% (12.5% from Year B, 12.5% from Year C, and 12.5% from Year D).

Each year, it became more and more difficult for the school to make up lost ground. By Year E, I&P Academy had to take out a loan to meet current operating expenses. Borrowing money from the bank was only another stopgap measure since the funds had to be repaid on schedule, with interest.

Four years down the road, I&P Academy had dug itself into a hole financially and was having difficulty extricating itself. Deficits sapped the school's strength.

Funds that should have been devoted to student programs and teacher salaries were going to repay the loan, plus interest, instead.

In addition, since next year's enrollment deposits were used to pay current-year expenses, that money was not available to invest. Thus, the school also lost the interest those dollars could have been earning, which further depleted the funds available for programs and salaries—a lose-lose proposition.

The key to remaining financially stable is to recognize your school's cash needs.

- If your school experiences a consistent shortfall of income, analyze the inflows and outflows and make necessary adjustments.

- If tuition represents less than 90% of your hard income, then increase tuition to provide greater coverage of your expenses.

- Improve weak tuition-collection procedures. Insist that parents honor their commitment and pay their bills on time. Their children's education should rank at the top of their list of financial obligations.

- Cut expenses, but recognize the potential for a negative impact. Will this action cause families to perceive that your program's quality is eroding? Will they leave your school as a result? Will your annual giving program suffer, either because parents are dissatisfied with the way your school handles its finances or because they want these dollars used for program enhancements, not basic services?

- Budget a cash reserve equal to 15% of your operating budget to provide a cushion for unexpected dips in income or increases in expenses.

- Make sure the periodic financial reports made to your Board of Trustees clearly identify any potential deficits.

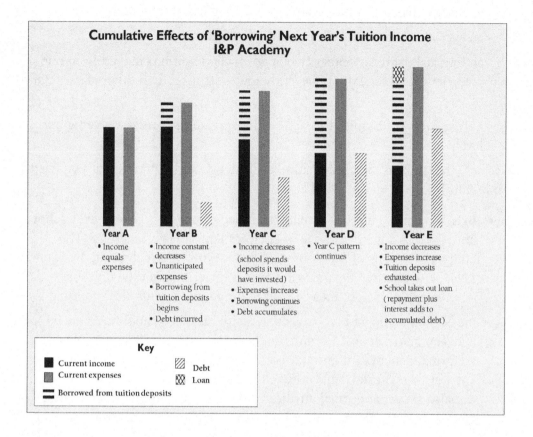

Cumulative Effects of 'Borrowing' Next Year's Tuition Income
I&P Academy

Year A
• Income equals expenses

Year B
• Income constant decreases
• Unanticipated expenses
• Borrowing from tuition deposits begins
• Debt incurred

Year C
• Income decreases (school spends deposits it would have invested)
• Expenses increase
• Borrowing continues
• Debt accumulates

Year D
• Year C pattern continues

Year E
• Income decreases
• Expenses increase
• Tuition deposits exhausted
• School takes out loan (repayment plus interest adds to accumulated debt)

Key
■ Current income
▬ Current expenses
▦ Borrowed from tuition deposits
▨ Debt
▩ Loan

Projecting Enrollments for Your Budget

Most private schools rely on tuitions as their primary source of income. But total tuition funds can be an elusive figure when developing next year's budget. You need to know how many students will be paying tuitions at what levels.

Your task is to deduct from the current enrollment at each grade level those who will leave between now and next fall, and add those who will join. You account for late entrants, dismissals, withdrawals, those not invited to return, those who refuse to re-enroll, those who agree to enroll once you have granted admission, and those who drop out before school opens. The number of variables calls for a crystal ball.

But your projections can be amazingly reliable if you pay attention to key indicators.

Begin by examining retention and admission data from the past five years. Carefully search for any patterns or trends. For example, you might see:

– a steady percentage of loss (attrition) from grade 8 to grade 9,

– an ever-increasing pool of applicants for your kindergarten,

– an unusual degree of integrity of a given class as it has moved from one grade level to the next (consistently lower attrition than other classes), and/or

– a steady ratio of inquiries to applications to admissions at a given grade level.

There are often universal factors behind such trends and patterns that you need to keep in mind.

- **Break points.** Families usually defer decisions to enter or leave a school until there is a major change in environment or class make-up. The built-in occasions of this sort are "break points"—largely shifts from one division to another, e.g., moving from a lower to a middle division. A lesser break point occurs as a class simply moves to another building.

  Break points impact both ways. If a nearby public school has a break point between grades 9 and 10, and you have one between 8 and 9, expect abnormal demand for entry at both your grades 9 and 10. Students may enter at your break point or leave the public school at its break point. You can also expect abnormal attrition at the end of your eighth and ninth grades (as students leave at your break point or enter the public school at its break point). You need to know the break points for every school in your area of service.

- **Last two grade levels.** Parents are reluctant to move students into your school from another local school if there are but two years remaining. If sixth grade is your highest level, you can anticipate little demand for entry into grades 5 and 6. And your own families are more likely to initiate a move at the end of the fourth or fifth grade because they know they will have to find another school soon anyway. Thus, enrollments trail off over the last two grade levels of a school, even when these grades are 11 and 12.

- **Middle school years.** In many communities, parents of elementary students are frightened by public middle school tales of alcohol and hard drug use, violence, and gang behavior. Applications for private school admission can mushroom under such circumstances. (Watch out though: These same families can lead the exodus at the high school break point.)

- **Local disruption.** The loss or gain of a major employer, the opening of an adjacent residential development, announcement of double sessions in the county high schools, or any similar event can impact enrollment.

- **Overwhelmingly positive (or negative) word of mouth.** It takes time to create a significant shift in a school's reputation. In general, it requires three years of enthusiastic (not just good) word of mouth circulating widely before there is noticeable growth in demand. But at that point, the market, if it exists, begins to respond with vigor. The same holds true, more quickly, for negative word of mouth.

- **Insufficient trust.** Parents don't want their children used as guinea pigs. If your school or program is viewed as new or untested, many people will hold back. Only those who have real trust in you and those behind the school are likely to enroll their children. A track record is important.

- **Single-teacher reputation.** In the elementary grades, when students are tied to one teacher for the year, the negative reputation of a single teacher can be enough to drive families away. Parents of students in the class below need to be aware of a change in circumstances before they are asked to re-enroll. Otherwise, you can project abnormally high attrition for that class.

- **High school years.** Once high school students have developed activities, friendships, some success, and a sense of belonging, they strongly resist a shift in schools.

As you make your enrollment projections, pay particular heed to your historical patterns. Don't be swayed by rationales that you may give for last year's unexpected growth or attrition. Lasting change is usually slow, so err on the conservative side. Don't fall victim to your own wishful thinking or pessimism.

Tuition Setting

All but a few schools suffer from inadequate funding. As a result, programs are limited or of lesser than desired quality, faculty must work at low salaries, or classes are much larger than anyone wants. Have the courage to charge what it costs to operate the school you want. Be responsible to those you are committed to serve.

Take the time to assess every element. Assign a Board committee to settle on what should constitute quality core programs and services at your school. At the same time, charge another committee to review your salary and compensation structure, determine needed changes, and estimate the personnel cost involved in the programs and services identified by the companion committee. Have both committees report to the Finance Committee and challenge it to develop a funding strategy. Finally, present the results to the Board for a decision.

Suppose your financial need calls for substantial tuition increase(s) and you are still gun-shy about a much larger hike than you have made in the past. At least go higher than you would otherwise. Test these theories in your own environment—then do the right thing in the coming years.

The Challenge of Setting Tuitions

Your Board bears responsibility for establishing tuitions. This is not an easy task. On the one hand, there is the goal of serving an identified market without excluding large numbers of families through prohibitive pricing. On the other hand, there is the goal of providing quality programs in an ever-demanding environment. In short, you want the best, but you are scared that setting higher tuitions will cause current families to withdraw and discourage prospective families from even applying.

The typical Board meeting devoted to pricing begins with a review of the recurrent arguments for tuition increases:

- inflation;
- real-dollar salary improvement for faculty and key personnel;
- cost of new equipment, resources, and technology;
- need for more personnel to improve services and program quality; and
- higher cost in several areas of general operation.

The focus is on the next year, compared with the past (known) year and the year currently unfolding. Discussions are influenced by what other local private schools charge and what schools similar to yours in the region charge. (Perhaps there is perspective on where your school sits nationally in a spectrum of schools.)

Board members then state positions based on their own experiences as business-people and often as parents of enrolled children—all to the point of what they believe the "traffic will bear." Many give anecdotal accounts of financial stress experienced by a few families they know.

The debate often comes down to those arguing for a minimal increase but agree to move to a higher figure of "x" dollars, and an opposing group suggesting a larger increase but acquiesce and agree to a figure that is $25 above "x." As if $25 per year is a significant difference!

We contend that Boards that rely on this arbitrary "seat-of-the-pants" model are not serving their schools well. Base the pricing process on many more and better researched premises than those underlying this scenario.

Erroneous Premises Employed in Tuition Setting

More than 30 years ago, ISM published a seminal article on the wrongful thinking often used when setting tuition. The article intended to help school leaders understand that pricing included a complex array of decision points, and that much of the "common wisdom" concerning tuition was incorrect. School leaders—notably the Board, School Head, and Management Team—must understand these variables to safeguard the school's value proposition. Let's re-examine four of the most prevalent false premises.

1. There is a "traffic-bearing point." Today, just as three decades ago, there is no clear tipping point where schools charge too much tuition. This truth is self-evident given there are thriving schools that encompass a wide tuition range. ISM often encounters schools that charge $10,000 per student and schools that charge $50,000—and every point between. And many of those schools have waiting pools at every grade! Three elements from ISM's research best explain the wide range of tuitions.

- **Price-Product-Process Taxonomy:** As pointed out earlier, schools typically compete based on price, product, or process—but not based on all three at the same time. Schools can choose on which basis they would like to compete, but it cannot be all three at the same time. And therefore, with an infinite range of tuition possibilities, parents can choose the school type that best fits their educational goals for their children.

- **Price Elasticity Study:** ISM examined the relationship of tuition increases and enrollment stability in response to market concerns during the economic downturn (we also discussed this earlier). The broad market consensus was that private school tuitions had finally reached the traffic-bearing point—the point where families said that tuitions were no longer "worth it." Our original study examined five years of enrollment and tuition data to discover what the tipping point was and when it occurred. This study's mathematical conclusion was that tuition increases were not having an impact on whether parents enrolled or re-enrolled. Something else, beyond money, influenced enrollment. There was no obvious tipping point on tuition.

- **Value Perception:** Surveying parents with currently enrolled private school students, ISM asks how parents rate the value they receive for the tuition they pay. Repeatedly, when parents perceive a quality education they rank the value as "high." Their high ranks, however, are not usually around academic issues as much as they are about safety and character education. Parents dissatisfied with education quality often report that poor academic rigor, a lack of faculty care and concern for their child, and low subject expertise of the teachers lead them to look elsewhere. Trustees and school administrators must drive value (meaning what parents see as high quality) despite the market taxonomy (or the price position) the school wishes to compete within. To drive value, a school's strategic planning process must always include not merely a list of goals, but a detailed financial plan that assures the school can afford successful completion of the plan.

2. Set the price we feel will be accepted, and then see what we can afford, given that restriction. This ignores mission and destines a school to mediocrity. The counter position should dominate: "What kind of school do we want, how much does it cost to operate, and how can we fund it?"

3. Only one year of tuition change should be considered at a time. In practice, most schools fall into this operational trap. Every December, the Finance Committee begins to develop the budget, trying to predict enrollment and budget demands to determine tuition. This trap drives value perception down. Let's be pragmatic—whatever your tuition level is, it's seen as expensive. The school therefore has to demonstrate the cost of the school is worth it. ISM recommends that schools create a strategic plan every three or four years, and simultaneously create a strategic financial plan. That financial plan displays the tuition increase necessary, holding enrollment levels flat throughout the life of the plan. This method forces the Board and Management Team to think about the overall strategic needs of the school in multiyear increments—and certainly drives value perception beyond single-year planning.

4. Our past tuitions have been ideal. Of course, nobody says this, but many act as if it were true. They work on an adjustment of last year's tuition, plus (perhaps) a small extra. The end result can be well apart from the real need; tradition has established the benchmark. Constituents have been trained by the school that education only costs what has been charged in the past.

5. Pay special attention to the prices charged by other schools. Be cognizant of others' pricing, but don't let it strongly influence you. Determine price by your own particular criteria.

- Your primary competition is public schools, not other private schools. (Look at the choices of those who leave or who never pursue admission after initial interest.)
- Other local private schools have different missions, characters, and reputations.

- Similar schools in the region have nothing to do with your price-setting because they are not in your school market.

- Never keep your tuition below another school's simply because of your inferior facilities; programs and services, not structures, sell.

6. We will base our measure of capacity to pay on our own circumstances, those about whom we are concerned, and those who speak out the loudest (the "squeaky wheels"). Rarely does a Board take the time to research the capacity to pay among the school's constituency. Yet this is the equivalent of "market research" for a typical business, and the information is not difficult to obtain. Specific data can be developed by a third party, such as your accounting firm, that sends an approved survey seeking parent opinions on many subjects. Buried among the questions is a checklist of income spans that represent gross family income. (Response in such cases is high, as long as respondents are assured that the school receives only summary information and that no data can be traced to a particular family.)

7. Inflation is the principal factor in the drive for tuition increase. It is a factor—but merely one. Keep in mind that schools differ from industries in that they are people-intensive and not "product"-driven. Education cannot offset the total true effects of inflation by increased efficiency—the classroom still basically consists of a teacher and a group of students. This corresponding lack of productivity produces an added two percent or more of inflation beyond the CPI-U each year.

8. Keep tuitions such that the greatest possible number of families can afford to pay the full price. This limits income, forcing inadequate programs and major pressure to raise money from other sources, while you effectively give "scholarships" to most of your families who could handle higher tuitions.

9. If we keep low tuitions, we can get those with greater capacity to make donations at least equivalent to the higher tuitions we need—and because such gifts are deductible, the cost is less for these families. Baloney! The argument is logical but does not reflect human behavior. You receive more income from a $100 increase than from asking for a $100 donation from each family.

10. Let's make only a token increase this year because we have taken heat for increases for the past three years. How can you not at least "recast" last year's tuition by the rate of inflation plus the 2%+ factor? You will dearly regret such token increases as you face price-setting decisions in the years that follow. Besides, the past resistance was likely rooted in the manner in which the increases were developed, announced, and marketed. Even large increases can find acceptance, indeed strong support, if the proper process is employed.

11. The stock market is in recession, so we should avoid any price increase now. We can find no correlation between economic changes and the purchase of private elementary and secondary education, strange as this may seem. Demand is too fundamental to be significantly impacted by an economic squeeze; one can put off buying a car or a trip, but a child's education is a constant need.

12. Marketing is expensive and time-consuming, and not worth it. Telling your story, reminding parents of the differences of your school from the vast number of choices (both free and tuition-charging) in today's complex market, has never been more important. The overall goal is to influence, to every degree possible, the conversations that happen every day—whether they're at the country club, the grocery store, religious institutions, or in your carpool line. We refer to this as internal marketing. The important point is that parents need to hear from the leadership about the school's strategic plan. Understanding why the tuition you charge is necessary is a basic component of driving value perception. Time and again, ISM hears one of two responses from tuition-paying parents when the tuition increase is announced: "Wow, that's expensive! I don't know how I can afford that," and "Wow, that's expensive, but I understand the school's direction, and while expensive, it's worth it and I want my child to have this experience."

See the difference? The first response is simply a visceral reaction to the price you charge. When you fail to explain to parents all the components of your cost, it's a logical response. Take the time to educate parents—helping them to understand the complexities of your program, the importance of paying quality faculty, and the valuable improvements to their child's well-being. Parents usually change not merely their response, but their conviction to "it's worth it."

Driving excellence throughout the school has never been more important. Understanding your market and parent perceptions about your school is also important. When you harness the power of these elements, you can build stability and assure your market position.

Announcing Tuition Increases

Typically, those involved in setting and announcing tuitions fear that parents will complain and rebel at any increase. Will you lose families? Will there be angry telephone calls and demands for meetings? Will there be negative feedback on social media? You need not worry if you plan your announcement in a way that highlights your reasonable cause for raising tuition—the benefits for the students.

Decide next year's tuition in early December and announce it in early January. Do not make the mistake of sending a re-enrollment contract with the tuition announcement. Give your parents at least six weeks to get used to the new figure(s) and plan their budget for next year before you ask them to re-enroll.

Announce tuitions in a letter to current parents, with a tuition chart. You will also want to create the data sheet referenced in the letter. The letter should be signed by the person who has the most "clout" with constituents, whether it's the School Head or the Board President.

Write a Benefit-Based Letter

The letter is your opportunity to give the rationale behind the tuition increase. Recognize that everyone expects schools to need to raise tuitions each year (and you should!). When you understand the way parents think about your school, you can draft a letter that not only states the price, but reinforces the value they get for their tuition "investment."

Simply remind parents that to stay even, your tuition income for the 12 months (ending in June of next year) must account for inflation. In addition, share with them the 2%+ rule on "disguised" inflation. These factors alone mean that to stay current in 3% inflation, you must recast your tuition figure(s) by a minimum of 5%. Emphasize the term "recasting." This is what you are doing: converting "old" dollars into "new."

There is no need to apologize for new tuition figures. Don't include statements like, "We are sorry to inform you ...." Give parents the essential parts of the data you used to establish next year's tuition. Stress that if the quality of your school's program is compromised, their children lose.

If you are going to increase tuition beyond the recasting, let parents know why the added funds are needed. Tell them, for example, that you have recast tuition by 5% and have added 2% largely to increase teacher salaries. Distinguish between the need for recasting and the reasons behind any increase.

Use the sample letter below as a guide in creating your next tuition announcement. Consider also the following tips as you develop your own letter.

1. Personalize the letter by using the parents' names—first names, if this fits your school's culture. A "Dear Parent" salutation diminishes your relationship with them. The parent needs to know that this letter is for her or him as an individual and that you care about him or her.

2. Ensure the tuition you charge is part of a plan, and the plan is transparent to your constituents. How you present this document publicly is a function of your own culture, but it should be accessible, e.g., through your website.

3. Tell parents about your school's finances, without belaboring the point. For many schools, tuition does not cover the operating costs—and the projected increase will not change that fact. If your school does cover 100% of its expenses with hard income (tuition, fees, and other billed items, this shows your exceptional stewardship.

4. Sell the value of the tuition increase. Even where you anticipate nothing new, stress the ability of tuition to provide the best possible faculty, program that delivers the mission, and various opportunities for the child to grow. Where tuition provides funds over and above covering inflation, you can really get excited about what's new and upcoming. What can parents and their children look forward to, and how will they benefit?

5. Explain how most students at the school will benefit. Parents have more sympathy for expenditures that benefit most children at the school, even if those funds do not directly benefit their child.

6. Let parents know that financial aid available, even if they don't need it. Indicate that any family that finds the increase to be a true burden is invited to apply for financial aid. In doing so, you reinforce for parents that you do not intend tuition to be a barrier to remaining at the school. This sense of "belonging"—the message that the school is concerned about supporting— must be addressed in this letter. (You may also want to send a variation of the announcement letter to families currently receiving financial aid.)

7. In the final paragraph, portray confidence and address the stability and viability going into the future. This should not be a "schmooze" statement. Focus on how the increase in tuition helps the faculty, staff, and Board better serve families, and how it ensures a stronger future for the school.

8. Create an enclosure or attachment setting out the new tuition rates. For schools with a single, schoolwide tuition, that figure can be included in the first paragraph. However, if there are any complicating factors at all—e.g., division- or grade-level pricing, payment plans, half-day options—don't incorporate myriad numbers or tables in the letter.

The enrollment form should not go with the tuition announcement letter. That document should follow two to four weeks later so that the discussion about money has a chance to die down and parents can make their re-enrollment decision based on value, not price.

Sample Tuition Announcement Letter

Dear (personal name),

In accordance with the strategic plan objectives for our community here at I&P Academy (see our website), the Board of Trustees and I have set tuition for the coming year.

Our tuition revenue (95.4% of total revenues) will support us in achieving the following primary goals.

- Ensure that we can continue to attract the best possible faculty for your children by offering competitive salaries. (This is Year 2 of a six-year process to enhance our faculty compensation.)

- Provide a full-time music instructor now that so many of our students (78%) are participating in choir, band, and orchestra.

- Enhance our financial aid to fulfill our mission call for diversity. (This is Year 2 of a three-year process.)

Please refer to the attached schedule to determine next year's tuition for your family.

Should any of you find next year's tuition a significant financial burden, we urge you to contact Mr. Fulmer in the Business Office to apply for financial aid.

Some additional funds have been made available for just this purpose. We don't want to lose families due to financial need.

Sincerely,

Scott Alfredo Medina

Scott Alfredo Medina, School Head

Follow-Through

After you send the tuition announcement, if you still feel nervous, you may want to hold a series of informal parent gatherings of no more than 15 people each. Coffee and dessert gatherings or "breakfasts with the Head" allow for discussion of the school's future financial needs and explanation of the data supporting the new tuition figures. For these sessions, be sure to get a cross-section of parent representation; invite some positive thinkers to offset those who bring a negative mind-set. However, in ISM's experience, follow-up gatherings will not be needed if the timing and letter are carefully planned.

Orchestrating Tuition Payments

Almost every school requires parents to sign an enrollment contract that obligates them to pay the entire applicable tuition, whether a student completes the full academic year. Some argue the loss of a student during part of the year does not reduce heating, lighting, or contracted personnel costs. The well-established position has been upheld in court cases involving loss because of student illness, withdrawal, or dismissal, as long as such conditions were stipulated in the signed agreement. Despite all this, most schools encourage deferring payment.

Also, these schools charge no interest or penalty for the portion paid well after school has begun. Typically, schools require an initial nonrefundable portion to "reserve a space" in the early spring. Half the remainder is billed in August and is due before school opening, and the final portion is due February 1.

If you operate like this, it is similar to a bank that lends its money at zero interest. The February amount is your money, but you are giving the family free use of those funds during September, October, November, December, and January! It doesn't make business sense.

Consider, instead, billing the entire amount (less the spring deposit) in early July, due September 1. Most people pay these bills shortly after receiving them, even though they are not due until much later. For those who wish to spread their payments over time, offer one or more piecemeal payment plans—charging, of course, for any such delayed payments. Many schools have been operating in this manner for years.

Obviously, the money collected before school opening is invested in short-term vehicles like CDs and commercial paper, while the deferred payments yield the extra dollars of interest and fee charges. As a result, you can more than double your short-term earnings. (See the following illustration.)

We believe the best approach to delayed payments is through a local bank. The full amount due for a student is received on time, part from the parent and the rest from the bank. The bank manages the loan, exempting the school from the bookkeeping or the need to harass parents about delinquent payments. (Schools despise being ogres.) And because the experience of such payments is excellent, many banks have been pleased to provide the service to school families at reasonable rates. If you want the service open to any family that you admit, you may have to stand behind the loans made by the bank. But we consider this a small exposure and well worth the service.

Full payment before the school opens also avoids losses because of "difficult" departures that you choose not to take to court. Likewise, those paying in installments write their checks to the bank, which keeps their checkbooks free from constant entries to the school—and increases the likelihood of positive responses when donations are solicited.

Although prepayment is an excellent policy, it gives a real boost to your budget only in the first year. Any variations after that depend on the rates available in the short-term money market.

A Simple Illustration of Extra Earned Interest

Assume that you now effectively receive "A" dollars in tuition by September 1 and another "A" amount by February 1. (The "2A" total represents the remainder of your tuition income once the spring down payments have been made.) Further assume that one-fifth of each "A" is deposited for immediate use, while the rest is invested in four CDs (each in the amount A/5), designed to come due in 30, 60, 90, and 120 days. The approach provides for a regular flow of operational dollars through the school year.

The average length of investment for the two sets of four CDs is then 2.5 months. Ignoring compound interest and assuming a monthly rate of "B," we have:

$$8 \times A/5 \times 2.5 \times B = 4AB$$

Now consider the result of receiving the entire "2A" amount by September 1 (as you would with full prepayment of tuitions). One-tenth would be deposited for immediate use, while the rest is invested in nine CDs (each in the amount 2A/10), designed to come due at the end of each successive month.

The average length of investment for each of the nine CDs is then five months. The interest earned, again at a monthly rate of "B," is then:

$$9 \times 2A/10 \times 5 \times B = 9AB$$

This result is more than twice the original earnings. Moreover, there is additional interest to be earned on the money received in August as a result of an early July billing.

Collecting Tuition in Advance: Aim for 100%

It is a Friday afternoon in late November. The School Head is in her office when the Business Manager comes in with some bad news. The Smiths have just withdrawn their daughter from the third grade. Mrs. Smith has been transferred to another city. Her husband has resigned from his job, and the family is moving in a week.

This is unwelcome news. The Smiths are the fourth family to withdraw children since the beginning of the academic year, and three of the students have come from the no-longer-full third grade. A review of the latest Admission Office report shows there are no students in the third-grade waiting pool.

Financially, the picture is even bleaker. Each family selected the monthly tuition-payment option your school offers. They all signed the enrollment contract, which included a provision obligating them to pay the entire tuition for the year unless the contract was canceled by a specific date. On withdrawing, each family declined to meet that commitment and expected the school to "understand."

Over the 10 years this contract provision has been in effect, there have been instances in which students did not complete the year and left owing tuition. In each case, the school chose not to pursue the unpaid balance. Using legal means to enforce the contract seemed counter to the school's culture, and the potential damage to the school's image would be worse than the lost revenue. Not only did the school lose money, but once an exception was made, that section of the contract became more difficult, if not impossible, to enforce.

This year, with the loss of four students in the early months, is a different situation. Of course, the overall attrition picture concerns the School Head. But the most pressing concern is the damage this lost revenue does to an already tight annual operating budget.

This is exactly the situation the school tries to protect against when it institutes a full-pay contract provision. When your school agrees to enroll a student, it makes financial commitments based on that agreement—hiring teachers, buying equipment, contracting for services. To meet those commitments, the school must be able to rely on the agreed-upon tuition income, even if the student decides to leave.

The following Monday, the School Head meets with the Business Manager to discuss ways to avoid future revenue losses of this type. What recommendations can be made to the Board? They both agree the ideal solution would be for tuition to be paid in full before the first day of school. Then, there would be no question of students leaving with an outstanding tuition obligation. But how can you take that step without alienating your current parents?

Your school offers three tuition-payment options. In reviewing the current year's situation, the School Head and the Business Manager decide that 65% of the families have chosen the monthly plan and another 25% selected the two-payment choice. Only 10% made full payment at the beginning of the year.

You both realize that it's just not possible to require full payment of tuition before school begins next fall. You're going to have to effect a gradual transition over the next few years. Even then, you fear that only a few of your families will be able to pay tuition in one lump sum. What are you going to do?

Currently, parents must make a $500 enrollment deposit, due by March 15, which counts as part of the annual tuition. Current payment alternatives are to pay the remaining tuition:

- in full by August 1;

- in two payments, with 60% due August 1 and 40% due January 1; or

- in 10 equal monthly payments due August 1 to May 1.

Your goal is to have full tuition paid, under all three plans, by August 1. You'll do it by gradually tightening deadlines over a six-year period.

The first step is to collect a larger portion of the tuition by increasing the enrollment deposit each year. For example, this year's tuition is $10,000; your $500 deposit equals 5%. For next year, make the deposit 6% of the tuition, the following year 7%, and so on. Ideally, you want the deposit to equal a minimum of 10% and a maximum of 20% of the annual tuition.

Second, design a plan for payment of the remaining tuition. The six-year transition will have a gradual effect on current families who do not elect the one-time tuition-payment option. The due dates for their payments are gradually accelerated and, with the monthly option, reduced in number.

At the transition completion, these families will have seven months to "budget" for the next tuition cycle—from the last payment due on August 1 to the deposit due on March 1.

Although the process is gradual, there may be families for whom the accelerated schedule will constitute a financial hardship. You do not want to lose members of your school "family" over a shift in tuition payments. While you see this move as sound fiscal management on the school's part, your constituents' primary concern will be how it affects their own cash flow.

Be proactive. While these families can take a loan from a bank, credit union, or other source, make sure you have information available on at least one tuition-financing service. Mention this choice each time you announce a change in the payment structure.

Look into the services offered by the various firms. Some will finance the deposit as part of the tuition (which can be important if you strive for the 20% goal);

others will not. Some work directly with the families, while others require an arrangement with the school before families can apply for financing.

In setting up this new tuition-payment schedule, schools must enforce it. Rewrite the enrollment contract each year to reflect the new tuition-payment dates and to reinforce the legal weight of the contract if you have not enforced the full-payment clause in the past. Then, if the account has not been paid in full, do not allow the student to begin classes in the fall.

To aid all families, announce the next year's tuition and payment schedule as early as possible, even before distributing re-enrollment materials, to help parents plan to meet their obligations.

	Option 1: 100% of balance due	Option 2: 60% & 40% of balance due	Option 3: Monthly payments due
Current	Aug. 1	Aug. 1 & Jan.1	Aug. 1 to May 1 (10 payments)
Year 1	July 15	July 15 & Dec. 1	July 15 to March 15 (9 payments)
Year 2	July 1	July 1 & Nov. 1	July 1 to Feb. 1 (8 payments)
Year 3	June 15	June 15 & Oct. 1	June 15 to Dec. 15 (7 payments)
Year 4	June 1	June 1 & Sept. 1	June 1 to Nov. 1 (6 payments)
Year 5	May 15	May 15 & Aug. 1	May 15 to Sept. 15 (5 payments)
Year 6	May 1	May 1 & Aug. 1	May 1 to Aug. 1

Enrollment Contracts Set Responsibility for Tuition

Schools often include qualifiers in their enrollment contract, stating that a full or partial refund of tuition may be made in certain circumstances. This may include, for example, catastrophic illness, transfer out of the area, or the school's ability to fill the vacancy. Don't do it.

Setting a firm rule on tuition liability is imperative. It is essential to come into the contract from a position of strength, stating simply the family is responsible for a full year's tuition unless canceled by a specific date. Exceptions may be made, but at the school's discretion, based on the specific circumstances in each situation— not as part of the contract.

Every exception included in the written contract creates a loophole that can be exploited. It might seem reasonable, for instance, that if a student withdraws and the school can "mitigate its damages," i.e., fill the vacancy, a tuition refund is in order. But look at it from the other side. Your school may not find a mission-appropriate student and attempts to collect the tuition; the family's lawyer responds that you just didn't try hard enough. How much time and money do you want to spend in court defending your recruitment efforts?

Case law supports the position that, when a school agrees to provide instruction for a specified period and a parent agrees to pay a definite amount for that service, the entire contract price is payable. This is regardless of the student's withdrawal, nonattendance, or expulsion—provided the agreement is clear and the school has not breached the contract.

By taking this position, courts have granted that schools are entitled to ensure that neither their programs nor the pool of potential applicants is subject to the whims of last-minute withdrawals. Schools merit this protection because they:

– must make commitments to employ teachers and buy equipment yearly, contingent on the commitments made by those who have contracted for the services; and

– have limited enrollment spaces available, and reserving space for one student may prevent another's acceptance. When the vacancy occurs, the second candidate may have already committed to a school with a more stringent contract.

Courts have rejected challenges to schools based on:

– being unconscionable ("It was a one-sided contract; I had no choice in what I was signing if I wanted the services");

– impossibility of performance ("We've been transferred and my child can't attend"); and

– unjust enrichment ("I shouldn't have to pay the school for doing nothing").

In addition, the courts have rejected the argument that a provision prohibiting refunds for absence constitutes a penalty. Rather, it is viewed as a provision for mitigating damages.

When a student or parent breaches the conditions of school attendance, the school may—with implied, if not expressed, contract terms—dismiss the student for cause and retain the tuition. Within this framework, the principles of fundamental fairness may rule.

Also, courts conclude that contracts for instruction are nondivisible, and that tuition cannot be apportioned. Determination of whether a school can collect full tuition or retain any tuition already collected usually rests on the specific terms of the enrollment contract. It may also depend on whether there was any wrongdoing on the school's part.

The case law mainly involves boarding rather than day schools. However, the contract principles govern all private schools—the foundation is contract law.

Schools also provide themselves with the strongest protection when they require full payment of tuition (and fees, if not bundled into tuition) before the beginning of the school year. If you offer partial-payment options, make the initial payment both substantial and nonrefundable to discourage last-minute withdrawals, and collect the major portion of the options before school opens.

Of course, there will be instances in which you make a refund. But keep the ball in your court. Firm policies put the school in a position to grant a humanitarian exception when, at its sole discretion, it believes the circumstances warrant.

However, be aware of any precedents you may be setting.

You want a reputation as a school that is both firm and fair, one that expects contractual obligations to be met but, under reasonable circumstances, will work with a family.

Charge It, Please

What do you do when parents want to put tuition or other fees on "the card"? Debit and credit card payments are an integral part of modern economic life for most private school parents, and they may be surprised, or even indignant, if you refuse to accept plastic.

After all, you can pay for just about anything—even a new car—on credit these days. Convenience, benefits (such as airline miles or cash back), low interest rates, and uncertain financial times may all contribute to parents' desire to use this payment method.

In setting up credit card processing at your school, consider these items.

- Some states reportedly will not allow schools to use third parties to collect tuition. Be sure to check your state laws as a first step. Usually your bank can advise about legal issues.

- You will need two items to set up a merchant account for credit card transactions, including:

  – a gateway service through which a school submits credit card transactions to the "processor" for a parent. This requires a secure connection from your school website or a credit card machine linked by phone in your office; and

  – a payment processor, linked to the credit card processing network. It handles posting transactions for authorization, clearing, and settlement to consumer credit card accounts at the card associations, and settling funds to merchant bank accounts.

While some services supply only one or the other, a "full-service" provider can combine the gateway and processor. This option is usually less expensive.

Before deciding on a credit card provider, shop around. Ask potential providers for an estimate of all monthly and annual fees based on your expected usage. Credit card companies charge various fees, some of which may be "hidden" in the contract's fine print. Ask whether all the following are included in their estimate:

  – application fee required for a merchant account;

  – set-up fees to process and activate the account;

  – gateway access fees;

  – discount fee to process each transaction, based on a percentage of the transaction's dollar amount; the rate is based on risk associated with the transaction, which should be lower than average for private schools;

  – Address Verification Service (AVS) to verify online transactions (sometimes included in the discount rate);

  – fixed transaction fees (as well as discount rate) for every payment processed;

  – monthly minimums as a "floor" on processing fees you pay for your account, which may apply if other fees total less than the minimum;

– monthly statement charges for your accounts;

– penalty fees if you cancel your merchant account;

– chargebacks or reversal fees if a transaction is reversed for any reason; and

– additional software and hardware required to make your account operable; this should be amortized across the first year's fees to parents to pay for the service ($200–$600).

If parents aren't clamoring for the option, avoid accepting credit card tuition payments and the inherent budgetary dilemma of handling the merchant fees. If, however, your school touts convenient services and programs that cater to the needs of families, credit card tuition payment may be an appropriate option. Here are ways to make it work.

Prepayment of tuition, with the full amount due before the opening day of school, makes sense in dealing with credit card payments. You can minimize the number of transactions and the resulting costs, billing, and record keeping.

However, many schools that offer credit card tuition payments choose to give parents the choice of monthly or quarterly payments. Like any other school-sponsored payment plan, this puts you in the banking and lending business—and often in the collection business, as well. As a policy, this is something private schools should avoid.

Tuition is your primary source of hard income. You want to ensure that nothing stands in the way of your school's ability to cover most annual operating expenses with hard income dollars.

If a family cannot pay the tuition before the beginning of the school year, then loan arrangements with a local bank or tuition loan service are the best option for financing the balance due. Bank rates are significantly lower than credit card interest rates, and it is sound fiscal policy to turn those who need financial assistance in that direction.

If your school is a member of a national, regional, or local association, does that group have an agreement with a firm that provides credit card tuition services? The fees are often lower than those offered by credit card companies. Compare services, rates, and fees to get the best deal.

You may be able to negotiate a lower service charge with a credit card company. One school, where 50 of the 600 families opted to pay by credit card, reduced the service charge rate to less than 2%.

For parents who do not pay the full tuition in advance, pass on the costs of processing payments, whether by credit card or check.

Be aware that, once set up, a credit card payment plan will be difficult to eliminate. Make sure your payment policy is well-defined and the costs are clearly understood before launching the service.

Re-enrolling Students Who Owe Tuition

Jenna is a delightful student. Her bright face makes everyone smile, her grades are good, and she's involved in activities—Jenna is a real asset to the student culture. But it's re-enrollment time and her tuition is seriously in arrears.

The Business Office has contacted her parents and they promise to pay, but only token amounts have trickled in. Still, her re-enrollment contract arrives. Do you accept it?

This scenario occurs all too often. Educators have an altruistic nature and want to allow every student to return; however, the Business Office views the situation from a different perspective. Another consideration is that "kicking Jenna out" would be a potential public relations nightmare.

How do you make the right decision? The simple answer is: It's not simple!

From the School's Standpoint

For a private school to operate, it must have paying clients. After all, teachers and staff expect their checks every month, and utilities and supplies are not free.

To ensure the school's solvency, the Business Office must set and enforce clear policies on tuition, re-enrollment requirements, and late payments. As we mentioned earlier, the most effective strategies for dealing with tuition are to collect most or all the money in advance. Or work with a tuition-financing service, which takes the school out of the "loans and collections" business.

However, if you are going to maintain a pay-as-you-go system, the school should at least require that tuition payments be current before a student can re-enroll.

Late tuition is problematic for everyone—school and parents alike. It affects not only the school's cash flow, but its reputation. The school cannot afford to appear lax when it comes to tuition collection on one hand, or uncaring about a family's financial difficulties on the other.

The parents' sense of pride and the impact on the student are also considerations. Usually, the situation is that the parents cannot meet the tuition bills, rather than that they will not. Dealing with this situation requires communication and careful navigation to both protect the school and safeguard parental pride and trust.

From the Family's Standpoint

Families choose a private school because they genuinely believe the school's environment is best for their child. Affordability, while a concern, is not the main decision-maker. Parents may decide to stretch and sacrifice to give their child this advantage—and may be unwilling to give it up, even when they cannot afford it.

Once a family is enrolled and in arrears, parents do have power. They can ignore your phone calls and lie to you about when they will pay. They may even spread destructive rumors about how the school is handling their situation. The matter is out of your control, and while the parents can—and when angered probably will—make the issues public, you cannot respond. The school's reputation is easily impugned because you have no avenue of defense.

Strategies

Working together as the Head and Business Manager, decide how best to carry out the following strategies.

- Make all financial policies clear—both verbally and in writing. Include them in the parent handbook, which parents agree to uphold when they sign the enrollment contract. At various parent meetings, review payment policies.

- Set aside some financial aid funds for unexpected school-year needs.

- Once a payment is 30 days late, make a polite telephone call rather than sending a late notice. Talk with the parent responsible for the payment, discussing in a nonjudgmental way the importance of timely tuition payment.

- Once a payment is late 60 days or more, consider that the parents may not have the ability to pay your tuition. Within the context of a personal meeting, offer the parents a financial aid application. This strategy helps you understand the family's finances and gives you the option of aiding with a discount based on factual information. Propose a workable payment strategy (including discounts) that leaves the parents feeling secure, lets them know their child is valued, and honors the school's written payment policies.

- If the family already receives financial aid, review the application, making certain that your award makes the school accessible to the family. Many arrears situations occur because the school or the family fails to accurately assess ability to pay.

- If you offer re-enrollment, understand that you may be "buying" a student through discount and setting a precedent.

There is no one easy answer to dealing with this situation. To maintain your school's reputation and to be fair to families who do meet their commitments, you may have to get tough with those few parents who are consistently behind on tuition payments.

What if your assessment is that the parents can afford to pay, but simply will not? Will you refuse to re-enroll the student? Withhold transcripts? Turn the matter over to a collection agency, or write off the bad debt? If you decide to re-enroll a student whose payments are in arrears, does supporting the family and avoiding negative word of mouth make the decision "worth it"? If you have built the expectation that parents can get away with late payments, do not suddenly take a hard line. Set policies, announce them for the coming year—and enforce them.

Ensure that you have a clear process in place, evaluate the family's ability to pay, and move forward with a clear understanding of the expectations for both parties. The school's reputation is enhanced when you handle these delicate situations with skill and tact.

Financial Aid

The Three Types of Financial Aid

Need-based financial aid involves understanding a family's ability to pay the tuition your school charges, and then negotiating (whether formally or informally) a discount tactic to meet as much of the need as possible. Understanding need, however, is a complex process. While we would all like a simple formula for assessing need, no two families' needs are exactly alike. (There are proper uses of financial aid or tuition discounts that are not need-based, e.g., merit scholarships, fine arts scholarships, and athletic scholarships. These discounts should be strategic, to increase diversity of various sorts at schools, and may involve the use of tuition revenues to adequately fund them. However, because these discount strategies are not need-based, they do not fit into the scope of this chapter.)

With this in mind, ISM offers the following distinctions to understand the differing uses of need-based financial aid.

1. Rainy Day Aid: Use this when a family originally admitted as full-pay has a temporary setback that prevents it from being able to pay a portion of (or sometimes any) tuition. This is often caused by job loss, pay cuts, a medical situation, or any number of unexpected financial burdens. Use this financial aid only to help current students continue attending through hard times. Further, the use of this aid should be viewed as strategic. It protects those currently enrolled and enhances stability for all students by protecting the classroom experience, not just those families impacted by a short-term setback. This aid is said to be sporadic—it is not anticipated that students who receive it will continue to need aid through the terminal grade of the school.

2. Aid for Diversity: Schools use this tuition assistance for strategic reasons—to create a student balance that would not naturally occur. Use it to add students of a wanted race, gender, faith, ethnicity, or academic ability, *but only if it is need-based*. This allows a school to shape its culture more closely to its mission—but only to the degree that a school is willing or able to afford. It can also help the school become more marketable, since parents expect an experience for their child that fulfills the school's mission. This aid is most effective when it is spread across the highest number of applicants possible, since the goal is to "buy" diversity. This aid is ongoing and, once awarded, you can expect those receiving it to need it through the terminal grade of your school.

3. Aid to Fill Seats: Use this need-based aid to fill classrooms, increasing the net amount of tuition income received by partial-pay families, which can add a significant amount to the bottom line. This aid should be considered last, and should be used when a school cannot fill all seats with full-pay students who are mission-appropriate—and only after those covered by the two previous types. Budgeting for this aid is difficult because its goal is to increase net revenue.

Many schools try to set one budget for all of their financial aid. This practice is inefficient and prevents schools from effectively accomplishing goals. Consider the following.

- *When using Rainy Day Aid, encourage parents to apply as early as possible.* Make certain to award these funds only to returning families that were previously full-pay. Understand that this is a difficult category to budget for, and use the net tuition revenue model to protect the school's cash position.

- *Spread Aid for Diversity across as many mission-appropriate students as possible.* The purpose of this budget is to buy something that benefits the school. Once awarded, you can expect that this need will occur each year.

- *Finally, fill empty seats.* The best strategy is to fill low-need seats first, allowing for the greatest amount of tuition revenue. Fill the highest-need seats last. Families that cannot pay any tuition at all should be considered at the school's discretion.

If you clearly understand the purpose of financial aid, you can then use it for the best benefit of your school and its students. Let's look more specifically at each of the three types.

'Rainy-Day' Financial Aid

By definition, rainy-day financial aid is meant to be a short-term solution to help a family through a temporary setback (e.g., job loss, divorce, medical condition). Strategically, this financial aid helps to create a sense of security for families—knowing their children won't be asked to leave without a chance to get back on their feet. Earmark funds for this aid from tuition, endowment, or a development initiative.

Many schools view tuition increases as temporary setbacks for families, but don't set aside rainy-day funds for this. While our tuitions may seem challenging, often we see a $1,000 (5% of $20,000) rise in tuition met with a $2,000 financial aid award if a family applies. Simple math tells us this doesn't make sense, even for a small set of parents that could previously afford our tuition, but now cannot because of an annual increase. In fact, families that have been at the school for more than a year or two should expect a yearly increase in tuition and should have made the proper adjustments to handle it.

A second or third child applying to the school is also not a temporary setback. Your school can decide whether one child's acceptance means that all children in the family should be accepted. But, unless you make a family with multiple children go through the financial aid process from the onset, you will not know when more children will need aid to attend. If your policy allows all siblings to come at any cost, apply the award to your diversity budget. Evaluate the seat under the following "filling the empty seat" protocol.

Another issue schools find challenging is getting a family off aid once awarded. A temporary setback should be just that—*temporary*. Often the issue is simply communication. When recognizing an unexpected hardship, the school should communicate its willingness to help and at the same time set the expectation that funds are limited and will only be available for a year or two. Specifying a deadline gives a family a goal and sets up an easier conversation about your intention to halt aid. Let a family know that, after the allotted time passes, their seat(s) will be evaluated differently and will not be automatically reserved.

If, after the allotted time, you calculate the family still cannot afford the full tuition, the family should go through the "filling empty seats" criteria. This only needs to happen once, and the seat(s) should not be safe if a full-paying family is on the waiting list.

Aid for Diversity

For clarity sake, let's break diversity into two categories. The first includes any student that mission drives you to accept—i.e., your school may be a religiously affiliated, with the mission to educate any child of that faith. In this case, you are giving aid to families that fit the mission but simply couldn't afford to come without financial help. Schools that have missions to provide specialized educations, such as gifted or learning challenged students, might also be compelled by their missions to help families financially that otherwise would not be able to attend. These are families getting aid strictly for socioeconomic reasons. The only interest of the school is to make their school available to families with lesser means to further the school's mission (e.g., educate children in the Jewish faith).

The second category includes students your school recruits to enhance its mission. Perhaps a school's mission is to provide a "world view." In this case, the school actively seeks students that fulfill that mission because it does not meet the criteria acceptably through its traditional admission process. This often takes the form of ethnicity, socioeconomic factors, religion, or nationality. Families should only receive aid if they have true need. Otherwise your school can be seen as treating mission-appropriate students differently because of their skin color, religion, country of origin, or other attributes.

Marketing goals simply involve searching for students in a particular category because you feel that their presence will make your school more attractive to future families. This can take many forms. Most often this involves talents, gender, ethnicity (i.e., "We have too many boys in fourth grade," or "We are looking for talented tuba players for our music program"), religion, or socioeconomic status. A school may have several different goals at the same time. For instance, a school may assume it will look more attractive to full-pay families if the school displays socioeconomic diversity, or if graduates go on to impressive universities. However, at the same time, the school may become concerned if, for example, there is an imbalance of too many boys in the early grades. After identifying these situations, a school may recruit students who would normally not be able to afford the school, to supplement an area deemed deficient.

Since your school may look to use financial aid to enhance any—or possibly all—of these categories, it makes sense to decide how much you are willing to invest in each category. If your school is strategic about using limited funds, be aware of where you are allocating them. The Board typically decides this after identifying from where the funds will derive.

Funds typically come from tuition and endowment—or you may use development to fund financial aid privately. Using tuition or endowment is the safest way—once a student has been admitted with need, you shouldn't expect that to change. With this in mind, counting on development dollars year after year can prove far less stable. Recognize that funding through tuition can have a great impact on full-pay families. While this is a legitimate expense for families to help the school provide an enriched experience, it can have a substantial effect on tuitions.

Consider a school with 300 full-pay students, with a budget of $180,000 for financial aid for diversity. The school intends to earmark (set aside) $600 of tuition per full pay family to fund diversity students. Perform a quick calculation by simply identifying the students that fall into any identifiable category. Add the total amount of aid of the students in that category, and divide that sum by the total number of full-pay students.

> **Total aid by category/Full-pay students = Cost to tuition**

Use this method to identify costs, to help inform and guide decisions for future budgets. Once you establish the budget, direct how to apply funds to carry out your goals. For example, are you looking for the most talented, specific-grade dispersion? Or are you looking to enroll as many students as possible?

Schools should be cautioned against using empty seats to supplement diversity unless families fit the strategic mission of increasing the operating budget. Doing so mixes missions and can easily steer a school away from fiscally responsible decisions. An exception can be made for schools that cover all expenses with hard income. However, unless there are always empty seats, this can cause expectations that you may not have the budget for in the future.

Using this financial aid budgeting for diversity, with rainy day budgeting, allows a school to determine strategically how to best spend this funding. This also ensures the best chance to create the environment the Board envisions.

Filling the Empty Seat

If you have already filled all the full-pay seats you can—and exhausted the aid that you set aside to buy diversity and help formerly full-paying families—only empty seats remain. So, if you have a family that can pay partial tuition, should you fill the seat? Consider the following. Look at empty seats as unrealized assets that have the potential to be worth the dollar value of the full tuition of all the grades remaining. An empty seat in the 6th grade of a K–12 school, that has tuition of $15,000 for each grade, is valued at $105,000 for a full-pay seat—i.e., seven years x $15,000 (no tuition increases are factored for simplification). Understanding the potential of the asset allows us to decide what aid makes sense to fill this seat.

First, let's cover some basic assumptions.

- Only seats that could be filled without changing staffing levels for full pay and the budgeted subsidized families should be considered.

- This seat should only be filled with a mission-appropriate student who couldn't come if you didn't discount.

- This seat should not be given to a family that simply wouldn't come if you didn't discount.

- The family's need has been calculated with a trusted mission-appropriate formula.

- For budgeting purposes, the amount the family will be expected to pay should be the original amount plus the percentage increase that full tuitions require each year.

In using these assumptions, you ensure that you are being responsible to the school's mission and operating budget. Now, having determined how much the family will be able to pay from assessing their need, use a formula to determine if, and possibly when, you can offer the seat. The variables of the formula are:

- *seat availability*—the total amount of years the student could fill the seat;

- *average tuition*—full tuitions from the current grade to the finishing grade divided by seat availability;

- *expected revenue*—the current year's tuition minus discount, or the amount we expect the family to be able to afford this year, multiplied by the seat availability; and

- *year likely to fill the seat*—the year the seat may likely be filled with a full-pay student, determined using recent history. Make this an honest assessment using what has happened instead of what might happen, e.g., there has been a grade that typically has demand for seats from a feeder school, and not just the memory of a student here or there that transferred to your area.

With these variables in place, use the following formula to determine if it makes sense to fill the seat.

Expected Revenue/Average Tuition = Total Years Paid
If (Final Year – Total Years Paid < Year Likely to Fill Seat)
Then Fill the Seat

For example, suppose your school has accepted a student to first grade and the financial aid formula indicates that the family will need $7,000 in aid of the $12,000 tuition to attend. The family is then obligated to pay $5,000 ($12,000 - $7,000 = $5,000). Your tuition is $12,000 for all grades. The expected revenue for the seat is conservatively $60,000 (12 years x $5,000). Using the formula, we determine for this student that $60,000/$12,000 = five years of tuition. So, *if* your school historically would not fill this seat with a full-pay student before 7th grade, *then* it would be wise to fill the seat now.

The number of empty seats should also play a role in *when* you decide to fill the seat. A family that proves it can pay a higher percentage may be awarded earlier in the process to ensure the revenue, if it appears seats will not fill. Families with higher need may be put into a financial aid wait pool to leave room for unexpected latecomer full-pay families. These families often have fewer options and are willing to wait for their answer.

Using this strategy builds your school's confidence when making strategic decisions that maximize the revenue for your operating budget. Ultimately, the process keeps tuition costs down and helps your school be less reliant on donors to balance the budget. How much it helps is as easy as adding the revenue for all seats that would have remained empty without discounting. This amount can be divided by the total number of full-pay families to determine the amount you would have had to raise tuition to achieve the same operating revenue.

Once given an award, families simply apply year after year. We rely on them to tell us when to stop offering financial aid. In reality, the school must calculate need, and only award if necessary. This understanding alone can add thousands of dollars in operating revenue (often tens and possibly hundreds of thousands).

Many families don't understand where financial aid comes from or what it affects. So it is crucial to connect the award with something they care about, motivating them to return to being a full-pay family.

Consider the following communication.

Dear Mr. and Mrs. Smith,

I&P Academy appreciates the commitment and sacrifices that tuition poses to the families that entrust us to help raise their children into successful, caring adults. We balance the need to increase tuitions with the need to pay our teachers and staff competitively so we may continue to provide the high-level of education that you have come to expect. We use a fair and mission-appropriate formula to make awards to families with true need. This protects tuition from rising too quickly as well.

This year, we feel we can offer to support your family with funds that have been set aside for I&P Academy families that incur a temporary financial setback. We hope that our offer to reduce your tuition by $xxxx will allow James to continue learning with his classmates this upcoming school year.

Please understand we use limited funds and often fall short of need. We hope that this offer helps you to quickly return as a family that can fully fund James' tuition and continue the experience I&P Academy provides. Doing so allows us to help other families that experience trying circumstances. Please keep us informed of your situation and feel free to ask if it is appropriate to apply again next year.

We look forward to seeing your family on campus this year!

Best regards,

I&P Academy Financial Aid Committee

Creating a separate budget for aid—and sticking to your mission of helping families through a temporary setback—allows your school to be more responsible with funds that come from full-pay families or donors. Respecting those funds must be a high priority.

Financial Aid and Competition

We've described the three basic rationales for financial aid. However, when schools are not clear about their appropriate rationales based on mission and need, another more insidious reason for financial aid creeps in. This fourth use of financial aid is as a competitive tool against other private schools in the marketplace. This deeply concerns ISM.

The scenario is a simple one: If a competing school offers a family $2,000 in financial aid, your school will offer $4,000—or even $6,000, if you want to recruit a student. In ISM's experience, this is often related to a student's academic prowess, athletic capacity, or some talent valued at the school. In the school's view, this improves the student mix, maximizes the ability of the school to achieve great results, and makes the school more attractive in the marketplace. However, private schools are in the mission business, not the used car business. Providing financial aid in order to compete degrades the status and function of our schools.

Why does ISM feel strongly about this?

1. *Private schools are not in a zero-sum game.* According to 2010 U.S. Census data, 10.6 million families have school-age children and incomes above $75,000. Yet, only 9.2% have children only in private schools, with a further 2.7% having children in both private and public schools. A zero-sum game implies that all schools compete for a limited number of families. In reality, there is a large number, and schools compete based on perceived value. Of the potential families with higher incomes, 88% are choosing a "free" public education—and that doesn't count those who earn less than $75,000, who are in greatest need of financial aid.

2. *Schools should not fight over students like dogs over bones.* When schools treat students like "bones," the message is clear: Money is the priority. The school measures the intrinsic value of each student in ways that are neither mission-appropriate nor respectful of human worth.

3. *Parents/families do not merely represent contractual relationships with schools.* Families, of course, begin with self-interest. Over time, however, the school brings them to a community mentality and engages them in the school mission. When the relationship begins with "bribery," however, the school and the family cement their relationship as selfish entities.

4. *Mission begins the conversation.* Teachers are hired, the school is marketed, donors invest, and the school exists, all on the basis of mission. Mission ceases to have real purpose if $2,000 of financial aid begins the conversation and defines the value.

A school's mission becomes meaningless, for example, when:

– a family chooses the school merely on the "bargain" offered;

– the school bribes through financial aid (and make no mistake that increasing awards to get students is a form of bribery);

– the Admission Office is ruled by fear of the marketplace;

– the School Head does not believe in the excellence of his or her institution; or

– the Admission Director poaches the exceptional athlete, academic student, or music performer from a competitor down the road by "paying" him or her to come.

They have all forgotten why their school exists.

ISM therefore calls on all private schools to subscribe to the following Financial Aid Code of Conduct. Post the Code of Conduct on the admission area of your school's website, and include it in your admission packet and other recruitment materials.

Financial Aid Code of Conduct

Our school mission is: _____
_____
_____
_____
_____

* Financial aid is one way in which we support families drawn to the mission of the school.

* Our school provides financial aid on a need basis.

* Our school determines need through a process that is equitable for all applicants.

* Our school does not manipulate that process to the advantage of one applicant over another.

* Our school does not use financial aid to compete with other private schools.

ISM believes strongly that our schools must uphold the highest possible standards of integrity. Integrity in financial aid involves having a formal process, applying that process, and not being influenced by how others use financial aid. Schools should compete based on the excellence of their value proposition related to mission, not based on financial manipulation.

Board Policy on Financial Aid

Your Board holds the responsibility for development of a policy on financial aid. Write a strong Board statement that sets the fundamental policy, based on your school's particular mission and budget guidelines—careful calculations of per-pupil cost, retained earnings, and incremental costs.

To develop an effective financial aid policy, your Board must:

- Decide upon the specific, mission-based purposes of aid at your school. A general policy statement could begin, "Our financial aid program is designed to provide _____." Each year, as you set tuitions and budget for aid, refer to your Board's policy statement for guidance. Although basic policy can and should be temporarily amended to reflect new situations, your financial aid policy should remain intact—something that a Trustee "buys" upon accepting Board membership.

- Evaluate the different types of aid. There are basically four types.

  - Loans: When funded by tuition, direct loans to parents will be paid back over time, meaning some return on your "investment."

– Merit scholarships: This type of aid is given to reward achievement, regardless of need.

– Tuition remission/reduction: Schools may provide this "benefit" to children of your faculty and administration.

– Need-based: These awards are given to a mission-appropriate student whose family cannot afford full tuition payment.

Your Board must decide what the proper "blend" of financial aid should be at your school, and have a policy statement that reflects that decision.

■ Specify the amount to be allocated in total and to each type of aid. Some schools determine the total amount of aid available by basing it on a specific number of tuitions—for example, 10 full-tuition grants. These 10 grants could then be divided into 20 partial-tuition grants, or five full and 10 partial grants, or any combination required to meet students' needs.

Other schools allocate a fixed percentage of budgeted tuition revenue or a percentage of total operating expenses. Most of these schools devote at least 10% of operating expense to financial aid.

■ Determine which application process your school will use. Families should be required to apply for aid every year. Some schools design their own application forms. Others prefer to use Financial Aid for School Tuition (FAST), an ISM service, or other financial aid services.

Most schools only include tuition in their calculations of family need. When determining need, you may wish to consider total cost—tuition, books, transportation, etc.—as many colleges and universities do today.

■ Stipulate guidelines for awards. They may be revised year to year, depending upon your particular school's situation. For example, you may provide aid by grade—"We will only offer aid in the upper school." Or you may award aid by a percentage of need—"We will award up to 50% of demonstrated need." Or you may even require all families to pay some tuition, perhaps a minimum of $500.

■ Develop guidelines concerning the acceptance of late-summer applicants for aid. If seats still need to be filled, marginal income is better than no income at all. Accepting late applicants can benefit all parties—as long as guidelines provided by the Board are observed.

Many Boards fear criticism from families accepted earlier in the year who paid full tuition and may resent the latecomers' "good fortune." Appropriate guidelines will quell those fears and keep such aid within your established budget for the year.

Your Board must decide on its approach.

- Give grants only to students who demonstrate need. Have your Financial Aid Officer process the applications the families would have sent to a financial-aid service to calculate need.

- Extend an offer to qualified applicants who were rejected for assistance before the school grants aid to a late applicant.

- Place a cap on the total amount of tuition to be "invested" under these terms, and set an upper limit on the percentage of tuition a given applicant may receive.

Offer these last-minute grants to students in your highest division only, to limit potential future obligations. In a PK–8 school, for example, a third-grader who receives such a grant may require increasing financial assistance in subsequent years; the new seventh-grader will require aid for only one additional year.

The Importance of Knowing Your Financial Aid Formula

Many schools complain that their financial aid often rewards families for poor choices—such as expensive cars, clothing, and houses. This is usually a symptom of misunderstanding how your formula works. First, you must have a full understanding of the formula that is used, and make sure you agree with its methodology. It is hard to defend an award (or lack of one) without knowing how the decision was made.

If you use an outside vendor, ask for the formula the vendor uses. This is what your school uses to award families and determines where your financial aid budget is spent, so it's crucial that you understand how it works. If you use a formula devised by your school, you should know who devised it and the theory behind the formula. Just understanding the formula helps you to better understand how the award you present a family was determined. This also simplifies the appeals process when a circumstance occurs that may not have been covered in the formula.

After you have obtained and understand the formula, decide if you agree with the rationale and how it works. Does the formula allow for "reasonable" expenses? Does it use what the family reports, or a fixed number? ISM feels that a mixture of school-determined and family-reported numbers is most appropriate.

Financial aid determination is about serving the school's mission and strategic objectives, and assessing a mission-appropriate applicant's ability to pay. It is as much an art as a process. Schools that keep these concepts at the forefront serve their families well and assure a reasoned, fair, and consistent process that supports the school's overall objectives.

The numbers for assessing eligibility for financial aid break into two categories:

– the applicant family's income; and

– the applicant family's expenses. Understanding these numbers is the key to determining how much a family can pay for tuition. To implement an in-house determination process, consider the following elements.

Applicant Family's Income

■ Wages and Salaries: Consider all cash inflows for the applicant(s). These include wages, salaries, tips, and interest income. Other nontraditional income sources include alimony, Social Security, grandparent (or other relative or friend) support, and income tax refunds.

Example: The family's federal income tax return is a good starting point. This will quickly verify most income. However, explore forms of nontaxable income carefully. A grandparent, family foundation, or friend may be available to contribute to the applying child's education. For re-enrolling students, an inquiry with the accounts receivable department often yields valuable information concerning who pays the tuition.

■ Total Assets: The next step is to determine the total assets of an applicant family. Assets include cash, savings, investments, home equity, other real estate, stocks, bonds, securities, retirement accounts, stock options, automobiles, planes, boats, and the like. Anything that contributes to the net worth of an applying family should be considered for income determination. Next, decide which assets you will use to calculate eligibility. Many assets are not easily converted to cash. Consistent guidelines must be established as to the amount and assets a school will use to decide what a family can and should pay.

A school may choose to exempt retirement benefits (dollars invested in 401k plans and the like, where tax penalties are charged for cashing in) up to a determined dollar threshold. Once the retirement account reaches the threshold, then, regardless of the penalties, income is imputed from the asset. Decide the amount of home equity your school will allow. Once that threshold is reached, impute income for the equity.

Example: At I&P Academy, the school's assets policy allows a family to have $100,000 in total net assets (cash, savings, home equity, etc.). After a family passes the $100,000 threshold, the school imputes income to the family's total assets by multiplying the total assets value by 10%.

One note when considering assets: It is unreasonable to expect a family to have no savings, home equity, or retirement dollars. They need these financial elements as they plan for their future. Families should also save for college. Equally unreasonable, however, is to give families a free or deeply discounted education just because they apply for financial aid. *The school must manage its financial aid dollars while balancing parent or customer service.* Schools can then systemically and fairly apply exact standards to the entire financial aid population, ensuring equity to all applicants and the school.

Applicant Family's Expenses

The family living allowance is an average of expected household expenses for "choice items" such as clothing, transportation, entertainment, and personal effects for two adults over a one-year period. Typically, these are close to impossible for a family to track, and even more impossible to verify. Even if a family can track how much is actually spent, there would still need to be a process to determine how much is appropriate. There should, however, be an adjustment for each child—the cost for raising a family with four children is much greater than a family with one child. With the local economies across the country greatly differing, adjust this number for the cost of living in your area. No single number can work for different-sized families or for different areas of the country. Once you trust the number that you determine for your living allowance (an allowable amount for yearly, everyday living expenses), you can stop worrying about what kind of clothes the family wears. Simply credit everyone with a "reasonable" number.

Schools typically make the mistake of thinking "Why shouldn't the families that are more frugal simply get credit for what's reasonable, so that we can treat everyone the same?" This thinking does a major disservice to the school as expenses like housing, insurances, utilities, and taxes can vary greatly from family to family, simply through chance situation and not frugality. Families that rent often don't pay for utilities; families with more children typically pay less in taxes; and families that have a teenager are most likely paying much higher auto insurance. These circumstances have nothing to do with how frugal a family is. Housing is often misconstrued as an indicator of how frugal a family is with their money, but this is not often the case.

Let's now look at three common scenarios.

- **Family One:** Bought a house 12 years ago and now have a mortgage that is well below the market average for your area.
- **Family Two:** Inherited a house and pay only homeowners' insurance and property tax.
- **Family Three:** Moved into town three years ago and bought a house that cost 30% of their earnings, which is the standard that a mortgage company would approve.

These three families will all be paying vastly different amounts for their housing. Sometimes the difference will be much more than your tuition. The question remains: Is this frugality or merely circumstance? Once you set your housing threshold for what is reasonable—say 30% of earnings—you no longer need to be concerned. You will only consider whatever they spend on housing up to your "reasonable" threshold.

Determine the thresholds separately for housing, utilities, insurances, and charitable contributions (if this is mission-appropriate). Taxes and Social Security —just use the numbers the family reports, but probably don't need any cap.

Here are factors to keep in mind.

- **Housing:** Consider the average cost of real estate in your area. This should be a fair starting place to determine family housing expenses. For example, if the average home in a given area is $230,000, the annual mortgage for that property at 7% APR would be $18,360, or $1,530 a month. If a family chooses a more expensive home, allow only for the average. This permits a family the choice of selecting a more expensive home, while giving the school solid reasoning for limiting an aid award based on that family's priorities. If a family owns a home that is less expensive, or has a large amount of equity and thus a small mortgage, allow only for the mortgage. For an applicant who cannot afford the average home in your area, use 30% of the family's total income as a housing allowance.

- **Taxes:** Keep in mind that families pay federal, state, FICA, unemployment, real estate, and sales taxes. Apply a fixed percentage to families for the determination process. This percentage will vary according to the area of the country in which you live, but should range between 15% and 25% of the total gross income. Make sure you verify taxes paid with the filed tax return.

- **Utilities, Insurance, and Other Fixed Expenses:** Contact your local utility companies to determine the average costs of utilities for a typical home in your area (electricity, gas, water, basic telephone service). Begin with that number and add to it the cost of health, life, property, and auto insurance. These expenses should fall into a range of $10,000 to $16,000 annually in most areas. However, be careful not to apply standardized percentages to these figures, as higher income earners normally pay a lower percent of their income for these expenses. This also ensures that luxury home and car owners' higher insurance premiums, tax bills, and utility bills are not over-weighted.

- **Long-Term Savings:** Traditionally, this has been a problem for many independent schools. Schools tend to think in terms of the parents paying as much as possible for their children to attend. However, it is unreasonable to think that parents should not save. Every school should have an operating reserve and so should families. We recommend 4% per year for families earning $75,000 or less and 6% for families who earn more than $75,000 annually. Savings, naturally, is a part of net worth. If the school has set asset thresholds, once the thresholds are met, the cash savings is properly considered.

Calculating Need

Once the income and expenses for the applicant family are determined, calculate the family's effective income (defined as available money after fixed expenses).

Consider this scenario as an example.

I&P Academy determines financial aid in-house. By policy, the school allows a maximum mortgage of $230,000 and has set a net worth threshold of $100,000. For a family that exceeds the net worth threshold, the school imputes income at the rate of 6% of the total assets. If the mortgage exceeds $230,000, the maximum payment that is considered is $18,360 per year. Tax allowance is 15% of income. The school allows each family 6% of total income for savings.

The Jones family applies for financial aid. The couple has two children, both of whom they wish to enroll in I&P Academy. Annual tuition is $12,000. The family earns $75,000 each year and has a modest home valued at $230,000 (the average in the area). Retirement savings total $30,000 and home equity is $20,000 (yielding a net worth of $50,000). The family reports annual fixed expenses such as health insurance (out-of-pocket cost), $5,000; auto insurance, $2,000; home insurance, $550; and utilities, $4,450.

Example of Effective Income Determination	
Total Income:	$75,000
Mortgage Allowance:	- 18,360
Tax Allowance:	- 11,250
Fixed Expense Allowance:	- 12,000
Savings Allowance:	- 4,500
Imputed Income (by policy):	0.00
Effective Income:	**$28,890**
Tuition:	- 24,000
Difference:	**$4,890**

Conclusion: If this family were to enroll and pay full tuition, it would have $4,890 a year total income, or $407.50 each month, available for food, clothes, and all other expenses. If this family were to enroll in a non-tuition-charging school, its effective income, $28,890 a year, or $2,407.50 each month, would be available for all other expenses. Therefore, the aid needed to enroll this family is determined by comparing the two differing effective incomes. It is unlikely that a family of four can pay for life's necessities on $407.50 a month. However, equally true is that a family should pay something for its two children to receive the quality educational program offered at I&P Academy. Therefore, the family will not have all the $2,407.50 each month available for expenses.

The best indicator for the award amount after the mathematical computation is family lifestyle. At this point, one must consider the answer to the following question: "How much can your family afford for each child's tuition?" The number the parents commit to tells more about their priorities than anything they say. While it is arguable the family can pay nothing, parents who offer $400–$600 per month commit a large part of their effective income to educate their child(ren). This is where financial aid determination becomes artful and the point at which schools communicate value to applicants. It is an important moment. The process that determines this "moment" is critical and tied to the mission of your school.

Understanding the formula your school uses to determine awards—and then setting reasonable thresholds—is the key to feeling comfortable about the awards you offer families. The formula may not always be correct, but you will be in a much better position to defend or adjust awards accordingly.

Budgeting for Financial Aid: The True Cost

When was the last time you looked at the financial aid line on your budget? Really looked.

Financial aid seems like a stepchild in school finance circles—too big to ignore, and yet, because its inner workings are carried on behind closed doors to protect the identity of families, never really brought out into the light of day and really talked about. And it is too big to ignore. For the vast majority of schools, this is the second biggest budget line, surpassed only by compensation.

What does that mean? Well, look at your own budget. It's easy to glibly say: "Oh well, it takes up about 10% (or 12% or 15% or 18%) of our budget." But in raw numbers, that translates into a big number. For a $3 million budget, that means between $300,000 and $540,000! Let's clarify what the impact of that is. A school with that size budget has 200–300 students, which equates to 20–35 faculty.

Given that the average faculty salary is about $55,000, what that means is that financial aid is reducing faculty salaries by 10%! That's enough to make most schools pretty competitive. That's just one possible implication. But there are lots of questions around this budget line. How do we determine what a "good" award is? How do we get the right people to apply? What are the ethical dimensions of financial aid? Is financial aid a competitive advantage—should we lure students in using this money?

Questions to Ask About Your Financial Aid Budget

Decisions about financial aid vary from school to school, and even by division and grade within a school. To help you determine what course your school should take, keep your mission and Board policy on financial aid in mind, and raise the following questions.

1. After total financial aid is granted, what is the net tuition revenue (actual cash) available to pay per-student cost? What percentage of cost does this represent, and how has it increased or decreased in the past five years?

Consider the following example. I&P Academy enrolls 179 students and charges tuition of $12,500 per student, resulting in total on-paper revenue of $2,237,500. The tuition-funded financial aid (discount) amounts to $264,000. The net tuition revenue (actual cash) is $1,973,500.

I&P Academy's Net Tuition Revenue	
Tuition	$12,500
Number of students	x 179
Total revenue	$2,237,500
Tuition-funded aid	– 264,000
Net tuition revenue	**$1,973,500**

I&P Academy's operating expenses total $2,294,767. (Financial aid is shown in this budgeting approach as an adjustment to revenues, rather than as an addition to expenses.) The net tuition revenue, therefore, covers about 86.1% of the school's operating expenses. Over the last five years, this percentage has decreased by 5%.

I&P Academy's Expenses Covered by Net Tuition		
	Five Years Ago	**Current Year**
Operating expenses	$1,835,813	$2,294,767
Net tuition revenue	1,670,590	1,973,500
Percentage of operating expenses covered by net tuition	91%	86%

This decrease raises several concerns.

- Greater strain is placed on fundraising and other nontuition sources of income.

- Less revenue is available for program improvement, thus compromising quality of program.

I&P Academy's Average Financial Grant	
Financial aid expense	$264,500
Families on aid	÷ 45
Average tuition–funded grant	$5,878
Tuition	$12,800
Average tuition–funded grant	- $5,878
Average tuition (after aid)	**$6,922**

- I&P Academy must determine the appropriate ratio of net tuition revenue to operating expenses, and make financial aid decisions accordingly.

2. What increase must there be in our financial aid budget to allow us to meet the needs of current families and new families we wish to enroll?

I&P Academy's current financial aid expense totals $264,500, which was granted to 45 families. The average grant was $5,878. Each family receiving aid paid an average of $6,922 of the stated tuition of $12,500.

I&P Academy's tuition will increase 6% ($750) next year to $13,250. Board policy states that for an increase in tuition, there must be the same percentage increase in financial aid. The total budgeted amount of available financial aid will increase by the same 6% to $280,370. The school expects 40 of the families who receive financial aid to return next year. What decisions must be made? Consider the following two scenarios.

Scenario I: Current parents receiving aid pay more tuition

If each individual award is increased by 6%, the average grant becomes $6,231 and the average tuition paid by families on aid increases $85 to $7,019. Each of the 40 current families receives a grant of $6,231 for a total of $249,240, which leaves $31,130 for attracting new families. At an average award of $6,226, five new students can enroll with financial assistance. (If the average new award is held to $3,113, 10 new students could be enrolled with financial aid.)

Scenario II: Amount of aid available to new families reduced

Since family circumstances may not have changed, each individual award is increased by the tuition increase of $750. Thus the 40 current families receive grants of $6,628 each, for a total of $265,120. This leaves $15,250, allowing two new students to enroll with the new average grant. I&P Academy loses three students, but "spends" the same amount in financial aid.

I&P Academy's Financial Aid		
	Scenario I	**Scenario II**
Average grant available	$6,231	$6,628
Current families on aid	x 40	x 40
Total expenses for current families	$249,240	$265,120
Financial aid available	$31,130	$15,250
Divide by average grant available	÷ $6,226	÷ $6,628
New students who can receive aid (at the average award level)	5	2

I&P Academy must decide which approach works best in light of its mission and budgetary concerns. One critical component in the decision should be the declining percentage of expenses covered by net tuition revenue. As mentioned in question No. 1, the percentage of operating expenses covered by tuition decreased 5%, from 91% to 86%.

The Board and administration must balance the imperatives of the school's mission with this disturbing financial trend. The situation may dictate a cap on financial aid at the $249,240 (Scenario I) or $265,120 (Scenario II) level, compelling the Admission Director to attempt to fill all remaining seats with students paying full tuitions.

3. What are the long-term financial effects of providing financial aid to a student in the early grades and "carrying" that aid into the upper grades?

I&P Academy has three divisions, each with a different tuition. Given mission, current classroom availability, program requirements, and faculty size and ability, the school has an enrollment capacity as follows:

Lower division	80
Middle division	60
Upper division	60

Current enrollment of full-tuition-paying students stands at:

Lower division	80
Middle division	40
Upper division	35

I&P Academy can add 20 students in the middle division and 25 students in the upper division without increasing expenses (except any direct costs for books, food, classroom supplies, etc.).

In this scenario, tuition-funded aid given to families in the lower division decreases the net tuition revenue (cash) available to pay operating expenses. On the other hand, adding as many as 20 students in the middle division and 25 students in the upper division increases net tuition revenue available (even with significant financial aid provided). This is the correct use of "discounting to the market."

Thus, extending financial aid to a lower division student may reduce revenue now, but that loss may be made up as the student moves up in grades and enters a division that has empty seats. I&P Academy must be mindful of the cost of financial aid over time, and find a balance that keeps seats full at the least expense.

No school can in fairness accept a partial-paying student in the early grades, and then dismiss the student later when a potentially full-paying student becomes available to take that slot. The financial aid commitment to a given family must be maintained so long as the student is mission-appropriate and the family continues to qualify for the aid.

As you determine your budget for the next school year, take a hard look at your financial aid program. Weigh your alternatives—keeping in mind the particular needs of your school and its families—and decide accordingly.

Tuition-Funded Financial Aid and Mission

Understand the importance of financial aid—it allows schools to fulfill mission by attracting and retaining students based on their abilities, not just based on their families' purchasing power. As such, financial aid is necessarily determined by mission, just like programs. As you prepare a budget for next year, consider how your school uses aid and how to handle it more effectively.

Your school must match tuition-setting policy with your financial aid policy. Increase tuition at rates that allow you to offer the quality, quantity, and convenience of services required by your parents and students. Offer financial assistance to those families who show the need—"discounting to the market"— and whose children are appropriate to your mission.

Tuition-Funded Financial Aid

Before weighing mission and financial aid, first understand the distinction between aid that is "funded by tuition" and aid "funded by other sources."

Tuition-funded financial aid simply means the student receiving a discount is subsidized by others who are paying full tuition. For example, if a given family's documented financial aid is 25% of the published tuition of $10,000, your school would offer a $2,500 discount and receive $7,500 from the family in cash tuition revenues.

If the same family receives financial aid funded by other sources, the $2,500 discount would be "covered by transfer" from another source (interest earned from endowments, grants, memorials, etc.) to your operating budget to make up the difference between the listed tuition figure and the tuition paid by the student.

Few schools today can provide financial aid "funded by other sources" to any great degree—and with current low interest rates, those funds cannot support as many students. No school, however, can afford not to fill every single seat with a mission-appropriate student. Aggressive use of tuition-funded aid provides a solution. Many schools use this form of assistance to students and, in today's economic climate, more should.

Purposes of Tuition-Funded Financial Aid

Financial aid serves both the needs of your students and the needs of your school. More specifically, tuition-funded assistance helps your school in the following ways.

- *Fulfill mission.* Financial aid attracts and keeps mission-appropriate students.

- *Strengthen marketing and increase revenue.* Use need-based financial aid to attract new students, thus filling empty seats and bringing in some marginal tuition revenue. Empty seats represent zero revenue.

- *Enhance student mix.* Financial aid is often employed to assure there is adequate representation from lower-income families (socioeconomic diversity). You also may wish to provide aid to other students who would bring something special to your school—high academic achievers, student leaders, or outstanding performers in various programs (music, art, sports, drama, etc.).

- *Meet current family needs.* There may be times when the parents of a current student, already struggling to pay tuition, cannot meet the next increase. These "satisfied customers" are worth retaining with extra financial aid.

- *Make up the loss of interest income because of scholarships "funded by other sources."* As interest rates have declined in recent years, schools have less money from scholarship funds and find they must supplement awards by using tuition-funded revenue.

Financial aid is a device to fill every seat with a mission-appropriate student without incurring added costs. Each private school should examine its mission, offer the full range of services implied, determine the annual costs of those services, and set tuition to cover as much of the costs as possible. Then, to maintain enrollment, the school should create a financial aid program that discounts to the market by meeting individual families' needs on a case-by-case basis.

Merit Scholarships

As competition for quality students increases, offering merit scholarships can be rewarding to private schools. Such scholarship programs present your school as one that values outstanding performance in scholarship, creativity, and leadership, reminding your community of the educational opportunities you offer. The higher the quality of your students, the more successful your school is perceived to be. Using merit scholarships to attract talented, mission-appropriate students can benefit your school in many ways.

- Merit students' participation and high levels of achievement in various areas can strengthen your program and help attract other quality applicants.

- The publicity surrounding the scholarship competition will attract families that would not consider applying to your school.

- Merit students often prove to be loyal alumni.

The increased attention to your school can greatly affect enrollment, not just in quality but also in quantity. Students of merit will apply to your school, and so will students who want to be associated with talented peers (or whose parents want such associations). Schools that have had merit scholarships in place for a few years usually experience enrollment growth in the divisions where the competition is offered. Many of these new students have siblings who also enroll.

If you are considering a merit scholarship program for your school, don't view it as a "luxury"—something offered only when extra funds have been donated.

Such scholarships should contribute to the mission of your school, and be considered an essential expense. Just like new textbooks, higher teacher salaries, and remodeled facilities, merit scholarships can reinforce your mission.

Keep in mind that organization is vital for program success. Select one person to oversee the program as director. Draw up your qualifications. What type of student are you looking for? What academic, character, and leadership traits are you seeking? What areas of your school do you want to strengthen?

You want to "raise the bar" and ask more of these students in the application process than you do of regular applicants. Remember, you seek students in the top range of those served by your school—in short, mission-appropriate students whose talents and interests match those of your current student body.

To be fair and to avoid ethical problems, make sure that scholarships designed to recruit new students apply equally to current students. Merit scholarships, if offered only to new students, can be divisive. Scholarships should be held by the recipients until graduation, as long as the talented students uphold specified, minimum standards, those on which the scholarship was awarded.

Promoting Your Program

You may publicize a merit scholarship program in school newsletters or memos. Explain to your constituents that financial aid awarded for excellent achievement is not diverted from applicants with demonstrated financial need.

Advertising your scholarship program to the broader community needs some creativity—go beyond the media that you normally use. Talk to local psychologists who specialize in assessing students and recommending educational programs.

Get permission to put announcements in their waiting rooms. Do the same with pediatricians. Put announcements in company newsletters.

Post your announcements in all branches of the public library. Librarians often know students interested in education, and may recommend your school to prospects. To help the librarians, leave your recruitment brochure with them.

Because your announcement will be distributed around town, make sure it stands on its own. Use the name of your school liberally. Tell what grades you serve. Give a short statement of your mission. Most important, tell how to contact the school for more information.

All the materials associated with the scholarship program should be distinctive. Have a special application and ask students to complete part of the application. Design a more extensive teacher recommendation form, one that seeks information about the qualities sought. Be sure to use a high-quality paper and have all materials printed or photocopied professionally, rather than run off on the school copier.

There should be special testing for all candidates. Offer several dates for the convenience of all. Besides a standardized portion, include a school-developed math test and writing section. Hold the testing before your normal admission testing dates. The interest in the scholarship competition will attract regular applicants. Charge a fee to cover the costs of administering the tests.

Once you've graded the tests, invite the top five or six applicants back for interviews. Each interview should be conducted by a teacher from the division the student will be entering. Have some prepared questions to ask all applicants, including some open-ended questions that require critical thinking. You want to give the reviewing committee some idea of each candidate's abilities.

A merit scholarship program can benefit your school, your constituents, and your community. Put careful thought into the application and evaluation process, with your mission firmly in mind, and for program success in years to come.

Tuition Remission and Category Discounts

Schools use various discount strategies, including tuition remission, sibling discounts, and full-pay discounts. ISM refers to these as category discounts, meaning that, because an enrolling student falls into a predetermined category, the discount is automatically awarded. This strategy can needlessly reduce net revenue per student and is a practice that should be reconsidered by most private school leaders.

Tuition Remission: The Benefits

No doubt many of your school's personnel have children of the right ages to attend your school. Do you offer financial assistance—either as an employee benefit or as a means to encourage these students to enroll? The position you take on tuition reduction can have substantial implications for employee morale and commitment, as well as school image and financial security.

There are three basic methods for offering reduced tuition:

1. **Financial aid:** grants applied for and issued based on demonstrated financial need.
2. **Tuition remission:** an automatic discount, full or partial.
3. **A combination of the two:** a specified level of tuition remission for all eligible employees, plus financial aid for any with further need.

Whatever assistance your school provides, the financial benefits go beyond the initial reduction; recipients also get a break from the Internal Revenue Service. IRS policy on Qualified Tuition Remission (QTR) states that financial assistance given based on need or in accord with a formal Board policy—whether full or partial remission, financial aid, or a combination of the two—is not considered taxable income.

There are caveats.

- This policy applies only to 501(c)3 schools and their employees.
- Any QTR program must be fair and not prejudiced.
- If recipients are employees of, for example, a church that sponsors the school rather than the school itself, they must declare any reductions in tuition as income and pay the tax.

According to the IRS policy, a school may make its own determination on who is eligible for QTR, as long as the policy is consistent.

For example, the school may divide its employees into categories (e.g., administrators, faculty, service personnel) and provide a specific remission level for each category. Or it may decide to restrict automatic tuition remission to a specific category or categories.

Of course, you want employees to enroll their children with you, whenever fitting. When they choose another private school or the public schools, their action can create the impression that your school is either too costly or not "good enough." (Of course, your school may just not be mission-appropriate for one or more of their children.)

Other benefits accrue when your school encourages employees to enroll their children and makes it financially feasible for them to do so.

- You increase your capacity to attract and hold talented professionals who can serve as important role models for students.

- You create a core of personnel and parents who have a vested interest in excellence throughout the school and demonstrate that commitment.

- These same people can help interpret for others in the parent group the demands placed on parents by the school and its programs.

- Their children can bring economic and cultural diversity to the student body.

Considering these positives, full, across-the-board tuition remission for full-time employees might seem a reasonable approach. They receive a strong benefit, and you are virtually guaranteed that their children will attend your school.

But consider the issue from a different perspective. Why subsidize families that can afford full tuition for one or more children just because a parent works for the school? Although tuition remission technically costs you nothing, its true "cost" can be overwhelming.

For example, if you grant full remission of $10,000 to each of 20 eligible children, the "loss" totals $200,000. And when you distribute some of that "lost" income to well-to-do families, this policy can be seen by other employees as limiting programs, needed equipment, and even their own well-deserved salary increases!

In addition, those who have no children or whose children are too young or too old for your program can resent the selective nature of remission.

Tuition Remission: Recommendations

The tuition you charge must cover the cost of operating the core programs and services considered essential to your school's mission. Based on that fundamental pricing concept, we oppose "giving away" tuition income through remission. Providing financial benefits to those who do not need them necessitates hiking tuition levels for others to "charge what it costs."

ISM has consistently recommended against offering tuition remission for the following reasons.

- It is unfair. Faculty and staff families with school-age children receive tuition remission without regard to their need. The school provides the tuition discount, based on employees' special connection (or category) with the school, outside the school's general financial aid process.

- It is inequitable. Teachers with no eligible children do not receive this benefit.

We recommend that your school forego tuition remission and use financial aid to provide for employee families that lack enough funds to cover tuition. They would follow the same process as other aid applicants, with two essential caveats.

- Employees' children should be admitted with priority, provided the class is not full at the time of application and the applicants meet the school's admission criteria.

- Financial aid should be granted to employees' children in whatever amount a recognized needs-assessment system determines to be necessary—up to 100%.

The latter should hold true even if your policy on financial aid for nonemployees sets a ceiling on the size of grants that may be awarded. In all other areas, hold to the same conditions that apply to others receiving aid—such as yearly renewal and acceptable performance standards.

This approach assures the school does not subsidize those who can afford to pay. Yet it gives deserving employees real priority—and addresses need to the fullest.

Many school leaders view tuition remission as a teacher and staff recruitment and retention tool, and a means of keeping competitive with other private schools. They also often view tuition remission as a way to enhance compensation in relation to public school salaries without increasing the salary expense line in the operating budget. Recognizing this, an alternative is to eliminate the salary paid by the school to the faculty member when calculating financial need, instead using only the spouse's or partner's income and the family's assets. This is a fair way to approach determining need for all faculty members and provides an equitable benefit.

In creating a competitive environment for recruiting faculty and staff, schools must address the issue of tuition remission head on. Giving a benefit to one group (those with children in the school) does nothing to enhance the school in the eyes of anyone outside that group. To recruit qualified, mission-appropriate teachers (particularly those who are single or who have not yet started a family), schools should place more emphasis on improving salaries than on tuition remission.

Stable schools offer competitive faculty salaries. Define "competitive" compensation as greater than the benchmark used by your school—other private schools in the local area, the local public system, your reference group (e.g., Montessori schools). Implementing this proactive position clearly distinguishes your school from the competition.

When creating a competitive compensation package and awarding tuition aid as ISM recommends, teachers with children will feel they can afford to work at your school. Since no bias is shown between faculty with children and those without, the choice is even clearer for those who would not be eligible to receive the benefit of tuition remission.

You must fully educate the faculty about the transition. If a strategic planning retreat is imminent, make sure this idea becomes part of the discussion. In preparation, with the Head and Business Manager's assistance, create a financial scenario that shows the financial ramifications—both in dollars needed to carry out the idea and in impact on tuition over time.

If you have recently completed a new strategic plan or are in the middle of implementing one, put the issue on the agenda for the Board's late summer or early fall retreat. Prepare the suggested financial scenario for this retreat, as well. Once the Board has adopted a policy to phase out tuition remission and enhance salaries, it will need to discuss how best to incorporate the idea into the plan. This may require that you reorder priorities, adjust implementation of a goal, or wait and make the idea the centerpiece of your next strategic plan.

If, however, against all arguments, you choose to continue offering remission, take these steps.

- Reduce it to the lowest acceptable level.

- Give priority to faculty members. They are the heart of the school and, among the various full-time categories, the group most likely to be underpaid. Providing them with an extra benefit makes sense, since they are prone to choose your school for the environment rather than for the pay.

- Weigh carefully the "cost versus benefits" of extending this automatic discount to administrators and staff, especially in categories in which turnover tends to be high.

- You can set your own criteria, as long as you are consistent. For example, you may wish to have remission kick in only after two years of service. Or you can "grandfather" those currently receiving remission and reduce or eliminate it for new hires.

Your Board is responsible for determining policy on the methods of tuition reduction and on which employees qualify. Include the policy in Board minutes and employee manuals, and make sure it is reviewed by legal counsel.

The announcement to eligible personnel (and those affected by any changes) should be made in writing by the Board President.

Announcing Changes in Tuition Remission

As your school's Board of Trustees drafts a letter about changes in the tuition aid policy for school employees, refer to the following strategies and suggested language, and adapt them to your school's specific needs. Make sure your legal counsel reviews the text.

The I&P Academy text is based on the most difficult of changes—canceling full tuition remission and moving to a financial aid-based plan. Keep in mind that all figures are for illustration purposes only; they do not represent an "ideal" policy.

1. Salutation: Address this letter to all employees including those not directly affected by the changes in your policy on financial assistance. Even if the revisions do not impact them, they need to understand the school's position and philosophy.

2. Overview: Explain the changes and the reason(s) behind them. Reassure employees that every effort has been made to ensure that the new policy does not create financial hardship for them.

I&P Academy text:

Over the past few months, I&P Academy has been developing a strategic plan to guide our growth for the next six years. Among the goals we set during that process are improving our fiscal accountability and increasing student diversity.

In going over the budget, we identified a policy that has a negative impact on both those areas. The tuition remission policy was designed to ensure that I&P Academy employees would find it financially feasible to send their children to our school. That is a goal worth keeping!

However, it is not prudent financial management to subsidize families that can afford our tuition. In addition, these automatic grants limit our capacity to serve others who, without financial support, cannot pay the cost of an I&P Academy education.

The Board has adopted a new, need-based policy for granting tuition assistance to eligible school employees. The new policy puts them at the top of the priority list and provides levels of assistance up to 100%. We understand eliminating tuition remission requires an adjustment on everyone's part.

Remission will be phased out over the next four years, providing time to make that adjustment.

3. Eligibility and policy: Explain which categories of employees are eligible for financial assistance and go into details on the policy itself and the steps you will take to implement it.

I&P Academy text:

Current employees: For all current full-time employees, the 20__-20__ school year is the final one in which we will offer full, automatic tuition remission. We will gradually reduce the amount of this grant over the next four years, as follows:

> Year 1—80% remission

> Year 2—60% remission

> Year 3—40% remission

> Year 4—20% remission

Tuition remission will be eliminated as of June 1, 20__.

In each of those years, you may apply for financial aid to cover the remaining amount, up to full tuition. Awards are based on need.

As a full-time I&P Academy employee, you receive two important benefits not available to nonemployee families.

- You will be given priority over other applicants, provided your child meets admission standards and space is available in the appropriate class.

- Once we eliminate remission, you will be eligible for aid up to 100% of tuition, rather than the 80% "ceiling" available to other applicants.

If you currently have more than three children enrolled in the school, the automatic grant will be available to each of them through the 20__-20__ school year. After that time, financial aid will be granted to a maximum of three children per family.

New employees: Tuition remission will not be available to employees new to the school beginning with the 20__-20__ school year. Children of full-time employees with proven need are eligible for aid up to 100% of tuition. The school will consider a maximum of three children per family for aid.

4. Application process:

I&P Academy text:

Employees will be expected to apply for such aid using the standard forms required of all aid applicants. For assuring the privacy and confidentiality of each family's financial conditions, only the Business Manager will handle the completed forms. She will tell the Financial Aid Committee only of the grand total of aid for which employee families qualify. The committee will, of course, handle such information with the discretion and care always expected with financial information.

5. Conclusion and follow-up:

I&P Academy text:

We designed this new policy to meet our long-range goals, serve the cause of equity, and allow us to make aid available to those who need it, opening I&P Academy's doors to more families.

If you have questions about this policy, please see the Business Manager or sign up for one of the small-group meetings this week. We've posted the schedule on the bulletin board.

6. Signature: The Board President signs the letter.

Sibling Discounts, Full Pay Discounts, and All Other Category Discounts

ISM has also consistently recommended that all category discounts be eliminated and that schools only offer need-based financial aid for the following reasons.

- Demonstrated financial need is the only equitable means for a school to give away money.
- Category discounts decrease net revenue per student by giving discounts to many students who would not qualify for discounts based on need.
- Managing the school's discount program is strategically important because maximizing revenues (and maximizing net revenue per student) is an important strategic component of long-term sustainability.

Transitioning to a Need-Based Program

Enrollment management is a powerful tool in building the overall value perception of your school. And a school's discount program is part of that strategy. Building value for the tuition you charge is a complex equation involving perceptions and is a process that school administrators must manage. Category discounts reduce the dollars your school receives. But not only do these discounts decrease income, they can decrease the overall impression of the school.

A school can manage this by using a discount strategy that follows a basic rule— make the school accessible to everyone who applies and is mission-appropriate, without awarding more financial assistance than needed. A need-based discount program therefore assesses the need of every applicant based on an overall program that treats all applications similarly, and meets—but does not exceed— their demonstrated need. By changing your discount program to a need-based one, the school transforms the discount program from one that reduces overall income to one that increases (or maximizes) income yearly. This program maximizes revenue and guarantees the school has the maximum dollars to pay faculty, plus build the best possible mission-specific programs.

Your school cannot carry out a change of this extent immediately. If a strategic planning retreat is imminent, make sure this idea becomes part of the discussion. Consider how to communicate this strategic change, and consider any financial ramifications.

If you have recently completed a new strategic plan or are in the middle of implementing one, put the issue on the agenda for the Board's late summer or early fall retreat. Prepare the suggested financial scenario for this retreat as well. Once the Board adopts a policy to eliminate category discounts, it must discuss how best to incorporate the idea. This may require reordering priorities, adjusting goals (if feasible), or waiting and making the idea the centerpiece of your next strategic plan.

Eliminating category discounts is a bold step to gaining control of your school's operating expenses and providing the financial stability necessary to ensure future programmatic excellence. This brave move, in the best interests of current and future students, is one strategy Boards must adopt.

Government Funding: Vouchers and Scholarships

Some private schools today, looking for ways to reduce budget demands, have turned to government vouchers to supplement tuitions. The Friedman Foundation for Educational Choice found that Florida, Indiana, Ohio, and Wisconsin are currently the top states in which private schools are accepting vouchers; 27 states have some variation of vouchers. Catholic schools serving inner-city and low-income neighborhoods comprise most of the private schools participating in voucher programs.

Choice advocates seek to expand further into the private school sector, but also place more emphasis on the charter school movement. Approximately 2.5 million students now attend charter schools, compared with about 300,000 students in voucher programs. Facing competition from charter schools (and other private schools), more and more private schools are tempted to adopt voucher programs

ISM has long advised private schools against accepting government funding—largely because to do so jeopardizes a school's independence. Research backs our position. A Cato Institute working paper published in 2010—*Do Vouchers and Tax Credits Increase Private School Regulation?*—concluded that vouchers "impose a substantial and statistically significant additional regulatory burden on participating private schools." In short, the money has strings attached.

Baker's Study of Vouchers: Implications for Private Schools

Rutgers University professor and school finance expert Bruce D. Baker conducted a recently published study titled *Private Schooling in the U.S.: Expenditures, Supply, and Policy Implications*. Here are three of the major findings.

1. The less-regulated private-school sector is more varied in many key features—for example, teacher attributes, teacher compensation, total operations expenses—than the public-school sector.
2. Religious affiliation chiefly accounts for these private-school variations.
3. A ranking of private-school types by per-pupil expenses correlates strongly with average standardized test scores.

On the second finding, Baker notes that schools that are members of Christian associations have the lowest expenses per pupil, the lowest faculty salaries, teachers with the weakest academic records, and the highest student-teacher ratios.

The Baker report deals with a comparable data array. But some of its conclusions are unrefined in their application to some private schools. For example, to imply (as in point No. 3 above) the per-pupil expenses figure correlates with academic quality distorts both of the essential points:

– first, that faith-based missions attract academically diverse student bodies at their intake points; and

– second, that faith-based missions, by definition, shift the nature of the outcome or measurement standard from one assessed adequately by standardized test scores to one more complex (laden with religious-character and religious-commitment components).

The Baker findings do not do full justice to the (statistical) quality of many religious schools and many small schools with lower tuitions. However, the findings do identify accurately a persistent problem with those same schools: low faculty compensation. While lower-than-market salaries and employee benefits do not always translate into lower-quality teaching—and while most teaching is undertaken in response to "vocation" in its religious sense—many schools fail to address the operations-finance equation.

Consider again ISM's "levers" metaphor—the relationship among net tuition levels, compensation, and student-staff ratio. The unwillingness of Trustees in many settings to increase (net) tuition to better support proper faculty salaries continues to plague sectors of the private-school market.

Too often in strategic financial planning, the projected tuition gradient is allowed to languish at levels that cannot support efforts to attract and retain a high-quality faculty and sustain a strong faculty culture. ISM has repeatedly urged schools to invest—via strategic planning—in its personnel, rather than in expanding programs and services. As is the case with many private schools, an unwillingness to allocate resources appropriately is a high-risk strategy.

The Future of Vouchers and the Price/Value Market

One of Baker's observations is that voucher systems, where set up, have used flawed financial premises. Funding levels have been so low that recipients of vouchers have been restricted to consideration of only those schools in dire need, but at funding levels well under the (net) tuition at such schools. That being the case, schools accepting voucher recipients have at times weakened themselves financially by enrolling students who were bringing with them public-source dollars in amounts well under the average net tuition per pupil. And this is apart from the related and perhaps even more damaging fact that, with public-source funding, restrictions and regulations inevitably follow. (For example, some Milwaukee Catholic schools were ordered to remove religious symbols from their classrooms and hallways!)

The Baker report contains interesting data and findings. From ISM's standpoint, the following observations are pertinent.

- Public-source dollars are unlikely ever to become "the answer" to any issue faced by private schools. Even if vouchers begin to approximate the full-tuition levels in private schools, the "strings attached" may prove lethal.
- The Baker report data call particular attention to the inadequacy of faculty compensation levels in many private schools. Compensation in the market does not need to equal compensation in the public sector. But it does need to be statistically far stronger than it is now.

The Baker study has reinforced school finance truths. The study provides a convenient reminder of the unforgiving nature of core operations-finance principles. Those charged with strategic planning in your school—Board and senior administration alike—should attend thoughtfully to these outcomes.

Government funding is unlikely ever to become the solution to any issue faced by private schools. As you develop your strategic financial plan, don't be tempted to accept vouchers to balance your budget. Accepting government funding could prove to be a fool's errand.

37573515R00077

Made in the USA
Middletown, DE
02 March 2019